BEETHOVEN

Da Capo Press Music Reprint Series

GENERAL EDITOR

FREDERICK FREEDMAN

VASSAR COLLEGE

BEETHOVEN
A Critical Biography

By Vincent D'Indy

Translated by THEODORE BAKER

§ DA CAPO PRESS • NEW YORK • 1970

A Da Capo Press Reprint Edition

This Da Capo Press edition of *Beethoven* is an
unabridged republication of the first American
edition published in Boston in 1913.

Library of Congress Catalog Card Number 72-125054

SBN 306-70019-0

Published by Da Capo Press
A Division of Plenum Publishing Corporation
227 West 17th Street, New York, N.Y. 10011

Manufactured in the United States of America

BEETHOVEN

A CRITICAL BIOGRAPHY
By VINCENT D'INDY

TRANSLATED FROM THE FRENCH
By DR. THEODORE BAKER

BOSTON, MASS.: THE BOSTON MUSIC COMPANY

NEW YORK: G. SCHIRMER, INC.   LONDON: G. SCHIRMER, LTD.
PARIS: HENRI LAURENS   SYDNEY: PALING & CO., LTD.

CONTENTS

ILLUSTRATIONS

LUDWIG VAN BEETHOVEN

INTRODUCTION

Only he who has never lived in intimate communion with Beethoven's art would venture to assert that the productions of the genius of the symphony present themselves under but one aspect, so that no essential modification can be distinguished in the course of a career which, opening with a few insignificant variations, closed with the five last quartets.

In support of the opinion which would suppress the division of Beethoven's works into periods, strongly marked though they be, we can find nothing to cite except a letter from Franz Liszt to Councilor Wilhelm von Lenz, the principal advocate of the "three styles." In this letter the celebrated virtuoso, after having first of all declared Beethoven's creative work to be one and indivisible, ends by himself dividing it into two categories instead of three — an entirely arbitrary and illogical arrangement. On all who knew the composer of the Faust Symphony and his refinement of appreciation this letter will make the impression of a mere freak of humor, or possibly even one of those solemn mystifications which, as a good romancer, he had a habit of bringing forward in his letters or conversation, with the greatest emphasis, for the astonishment of reader or auditor, thereafter laughing over them in private. At all events, if such was his view in 1852, he professed twenty years later an opinion diametrically opposed, when it was our privilege to dwell near him in Weimar, and when he uttered such judicious remarks on the subject of the *three Beethovens:* "the child, the man, the god." Hence, no serious criticism would attach to the document in question any greater importance than to the dogmatic pronouncements of those "Wagnerizers" who decreed, about the year 1890, the absolute artistic identity of *Parsifal, Tannhäuser,* and — *Rienzi.*

It appears certain that the career of every creative artist, whose life attains normal duration, divides into three periods differing one from the other in the character of the compositions: Imitation, transition, reflection.

In the first period, after having studied more or less at length the rules and traditional processes of the trade, the artist will imitate. Not one of the grand pioneers in poetry, painting or music has evaded this law — an Alighieri no more than a Molière, a Gozzoli no more than a Rembrandt, a Bach no more than a Wagner. Before this law the too-convenient theory of autodidactic geniuses falls to the ground — a theory of which, it must be admitted, the history of art offers not a single example.

Following this period of imitation, whose duration varies with different composers (in Beethoven's case it occupied eight years of his life), the young artist gradually frees himself from his leading-strings. He tries to walk alone. Then, with an increasingly vivid consciousness of the joyous or sorrowful movements of his soul, it is *himself* that he seeks, not without hesitations and gropings, to express in his art.

With some, like Bach or Haydn, it will be the tranquillity of the trusting soul (Allemande of the Fourth Partita for harpsichord, by Bach), or mayhap a wholesome gayety bordering on roguishness (Haydn's finales). With others

(Beethoven, for example) it will be poignant passion, or the feeling of rural calm; with all it will be the attempt to make manifest, in their works, the emotions created in the soul by the events of life. A period more especially human, to put it correctly, a period in which external procedure, execution, occupies a large place, a period preparing for the artist the way to a definitive eclosion of his personality.

To this manner would seem to belong (to mention only a few works) the *Convivio* of Dante, the *Night-Watch* of Rembrandt, the chamber concertos of Bach, *Tristan* by Wagner.

And finally, when the man of genius, weary of expressing his own joys and his own sorrows, disdainful or careless of his environment, shall concentrate within himself his incessant aspiration after pure beauty, the instant has arrived, for men of highest stature, for the supreme transformation, the time for works of pure Art, of Faith and of Love.

Such are Dante's *Divine Comedy*, Fra Angelico's frescos in the chapel of Nicholas V., Rembrandt's *Syndics*, Bach's Mass in *B* minor, Richard Wagner's *Parsifal*.

In the above we have outlined the productive life-history of almost all, not to say all, those men who are worthy to be called artistic geniuses. In not one among them can these various transformations be traced more readily than in Beethoven, by a study of their works, and, so to speak, step by step. We shall make this study — restricted perforce to an examination of the most characteristic works — the object of the following pages.

THE FIRST PERIOD

UNTIL 1801

I

HIS LIFE

IN Bonn that evening there was a festival at number 934 of the narrow street which is called the *Rheingasse* (Rhine Alley). In the Beethovens' dwelling they were celebrating the day of Mary Magdalen in honor of the mistress of the house, *née* Maria Magdalena Keverich, and quite a number of musicians belonging to the Electoral Kapelle were gathered together in the home of the court tenor, their comrade Johann van Beethoven, to aid him in regaling his guests with a little music interspersed with grilled sausages, refreshments and merry talk.

In the "best room" (*gute Stube*) a harpsichord and music-desks have been ranged in order. Under the canopy adorned with foliage, where Frau van Beethoven is about to take her place, appears in a gilt frame the portrait of Kapellmeister Ludwig van Beethoven, the household *Lar*, the illustrious man of the family.*

Radoux, portrait-painter to the Court, depicted him in life-size, clad in a fur cloak with a long-sleeved over-mantle,

* It was through him that the Beethoven family traced their connection with that Netherlandish homeland whence they were brought by the whim of an ecclesiastical Mæcenas, Clement Augustus, Prince-Elector of Cologne. Kapellmeister Ludwig, born at Antwerp in 1712, was the descendant of a line of artists among whom were numbered painters and sculptors.

[4]

seated in an armchair, a velvet cap with gold tassel on his head, a roll of music in his hand; in general appearance a small man with broad forehead, keen eyes and dark complexion. At the harpsichord sits another Ludwig. It is the oldest of his grandchildren, a boy barely eight years of age (he was born the 16th of December, 1770), who is making ready to play a sonata by Mozart or Ph. Emanuel Bach under the kindly eyes of the musicians of his company — Reicha, Ries, Simrock, the Rombergs, the actor Lux, etc. His slender frame and short legs seem to find difficulty in supporting an enormous head which one might fancy descended out of the rejuvenated portrait. He, too, has the black hair and dark complexion which are to earn him the sobriquet of "the Spaniard." His precocious talents already promise a new link in the unbroken chain of Kapellmeister.

Nearby, tenderly gazing on him, we see Frau van Beethoven, still young and pretty, albeit somewhat faded. A daughter of respectable burgher-folk — her father was chief cook to the Prince-Elector — this excellent housewife, who is at the same time a woman of distinction, "can suitably conform her speech to the humblest and to the most exalted personages." She is idolized by the three little boys, Ludwig, Carl and Johann; and, although her husband inherited from his mother's side an immoderate liking for the juice of his Rhenish grapes, no disputes have disturbed the harmony of the household. Later, when she dies of consumption, the father will fall, a hopeless wreck; and the youthful Ludwig, in a celebrated letter, will pour out the first affliction of his heart, of that "heart in which everything reëchoes."*

---

* All passages in quotation-marks are authentic citations from Beethoven's spoken or written words, without further indication of their sources.

In a corner of the room a monk is listening most attentively to the family concert. It is an organist, Father Hanzmann, who never fails to appear at these reunions. With the Franciscan brother, Willibald Koch, he divides the honor of having been one of Beethoven's first organ-teachers.

Lastly, in the background, a tall, handsome man of elongated visage and somewhat severe mien, a powdered periwig on his head — the father of the family.

Such is the tableau handed down to us by goodman Fischer,* the family baker and caterer to the corporation of musicians, who, in this capacity, was sometimes invited to join the friends. A far different picture, it must be admitted, from that exhibited to us by romantic writers a trifle over-wrought by a passion for the dark side of life. Instead of a Beethoven maltreated and beaten, always in tears, we see a child energetically urged to work by his father, who recognized his great abilities and who, with very pardonable pride, produced him at a concert as even younger than he was.

The child was, in very truth, a dreamer; neighbors who came to listen beneath the window might often have seen him lost in contemplation of the broad Rhine and the Seven Mountains. But, aside from this, he enjoyed and found time for the pranks of youth; unhooking the landlord's blinds to make them creak, purloining Mother Fischer's eggs ("I am only a note-snatcher," he laughingly replied when accused of being an egg-snatcher), or wandering in vacation-time through his beloved country, and picking up here and there certain fieldfare-pies wherewith the curates

* See the MS. by Fischer in the Beethoven House at Bonn; and *cf.* Thayer's Biography, second edition (German), Vol. I, pp. 117–125, and the Suppl., VII, pp. 415–448.

SILHOUETTE OF BEETHOVEN, AGED SIXTEEN

ORGAN AT THE MONASTERY OF THE MINORITES, IN BONN, WHERE
BEETHOVEN LEARNED TO PLAY
(Beethoven Museum, Bonn)

of the neighborhood would regale him in recompense for an improvisation on the organ.

His first instructors were his cousin, the pious Rovantini, kindliness itself; Pfeiffer, whose alleged ill-treatment left no bitterness in his pupil's spirit, since the latter did not hesitate, some years later, to aid his old master in time of need; and Neefe, the court organist, who had made of the little virtuoso, *the young amateur, aged twelve,* his deputy in the Electoral chapel. Thanks to him, Beethoven will soon occupy a salaried position bringing in 150 florins. And then, how proud was his father to escort the little gentleman of a Sunday through the streets of Bonn in his gala costume: — a light green coat, a vest of embroidered silk with great gold-fringed pockets, a shirt-frill that threatened to throttle him, and a well-dressed peruke underneath which his rebellious hair could hardly be kept quiet.

How great his satisfaction to hear Ludwig improvise audaciously on the theme of the *Credo*, or amuse himself by "throwing out" a famous singer in the Lamentations of Jeremiah — to the vast delight of his comrades!

And thus it came that the young man always remained grateful to his true initiator into musical art, Neefe; a man of cultivation, a philosopher when the spirit moved, but above all a farseeing pedagogue. "If I ever become anybody," Beethoven wrote him, "I shall owe it to you."

Before the eyes of the future composer Neefe unrolled the entire contents of his well-stocked musical library — German, French and Italian works. But to the theoretical study of the forms he wished Beethoven to add practical routine; he made him practise the preludes and fugues of the "Well-tempered Clavichord" from the age of thirteen; to him, in his capacity of chorus-rehearser, he entrusted the accompaniment at the cembalo from the bass of opera-scores; he procured him the appointment of tenor-player in the orchestra, through which Beethoven obtained his profound knowledge of instrumentation.

While the artistic formation of the young musician went on rapidly in such contact, the influences of the environment into which he was necessarily thrown might, perhaps, have tainted his mind and heart; but, as von Lenz says, "God watched over the soul to which he had confided the revelation to men of the Pastoral Symphony."

Observe, beneath the lindens in the square by the church, this mansion surrounded by a lattice laden with climbing roses. Behind the snowy curtains of muslin dwell peace and well-being; it is the family mansion of the Breunings — to become maternal for Beethoven, now that he is acquainted with grief.

We are in 1787; Frau van Beethoven is dead; the father, delivered over by sorrow to his unhappy propensity, can no longer be a guide for the youthful Ludwig. In this mansion the latter is to regain, as it were, a vision of the past. Here they make music, and likewise pursue literature and philosophy, under the serious eye of the widow of archivist von Breuning. "She was my guardian angel!" writes Beethoven at a later date. His friend Wegeler, the future husband of Eleonore, introduced him into this home whose hospitality he will be so eager to seek. Little Eleonore amuses herself with writing verses when not embroidering by the lamp, and her uncles, the canons Lorenz and Philipp, read Klopstock to the young people while awaiting the entry of violin and harpsichord.

How the poor orphan's heart is warmed, close to these choice spirits, who, in the sequel, understood and loved him, yet without flattering him! "Frau von Breuning," as Beethoven said later, "knew how to remove noxious insects from the bud." She inculcated industry and modesty, while the children assisted in giving the musician that educational polish which is observable in his letters to princely personages.

In the town of Bonn, where the lessons given by his father were appreciated, he already had the latter's entire aristocratic clientèle — the Hatzfelds, the Honraths, the Westerholdts. And now an unhoped-for opportunity brings about a meeting here with one who is to give a decisive impulse to his vocation.

Count Waldstein, a guest at the Breunings, found himself strongly inclined, through similarity of age and tastes, to friendly intimacy with the artist. He had been struck by the manner in which the young man could evolve *musical portraits* at the harpsichord — a recreation equally admired at the Breunings' with the cutting out of silhouettes; he had admired young Ludwig's expressive playing and his peculiar way of attacking the keyboard. He insisted on presenting him his first grand piano, and the visits of the charming *grand seigneur* to the humble room in the Wenzelgasse were numbered among Beethoven's most cherished remembrances of Bonn.

By means of all these connections the young man's renown grows and strengthens; people begin to talk about the concerts he gives at Court. Waldstein has ordered of him a "Ritter-Ballett" and variations on a theme of his own. Beethoven composes occasional cantatas for the death and coronation of the emperors of Austria, brothers of his Prince-Bishop. Max Franz, like his sister Marie-Antoinette, a protector of artists, takes increasing interest in the rising star: for did not Mozart say of him, "he will make a noise in the world some day?" And "Papa Haydn," passing through Bonn on his way home from England — was he not surprised at seeing him still a provincial, remote from the advice of the masters?

And so, at the instance of Neefe and Waldstein, the Prince-Elector decided to deprive himself of the services of his favorite concert-player, and to send him with a stipend to Vienna to finish his studies under Haydn.

What a commotion in the little town — their great man is about to depart! And they vie with each other in bringing Beethoven souvenirs, drawings, mottoes for his album. Everybody, down to the sacristan of the electoral chapel, wants to figure on this precious roll of friends.

Meantime, Waldstein has provided his friend with numerous letters of introduction, and used his influence to open to him the salons of the high Viennese aristocracy, of Fries, Liechtenstein, Schwarzenberg. We shall soon see Beethoven on a familiar footing with Prince Lichnowsky, with an annuity of 600 florins, and a servant under orders to answer his (Beethoven's) bell rather than that of the Prince. We shall assist at his essays in "sport" on the horse offered him by General von Browne; a countess of Thun, the mother of the "three Graces," will kneel before him to persuade him to take his seat at the piano; Baron Pasqualati, of whose misery he is to sing so magnificently, will bear with the caprices of his lodger, such as piercing the walls, or ablutions bringing disaster to the parquet flooring. Beethoven will have his summer lodgings, whither he will transport himself at great expense with his grand piano and all sorts of cumbersome objects, like cages for poultry, etc. The empress, to whom he will dedicate his Septet, will assist at his concerts; and finally he will become a commensal official of Archduke Charles, and instructor and friend of the emperor's youngest brother, the "dear little Archduke" Rudolph.

Just now, however, our hero, transplanted to Vienna, has not reached this point; he rather cuts the figure of a great man from the provinces in the capital, something like Lucien de Rubempré, only lacking (alas!) his beauty. And he always looks unkempt. His low stature, his over-ruddy face, his morose mien, his mirth-provoking Rhenish accent, his untidy garb, wrest from his earlier comrade in Bonn, the actress Magdalena Willmann, the heartfelt outcry, "I won't marry him! he is too ugly, and half-crazy!"

Were it not for his eyes, whose unforgetable expression illumines his countenance, there would of a surety be nothing seductive about the man. And yet, one has only to know him to love him; his brusque exterior hides a heart of gold. After his father's death he helped his brothers establish themselves, the one as an official in Vienna, the other as an apothecary. And should some poor devil of a musician happen upon hard times, Beethoven will seek him out with open hand; he even finds leisure to give lessons to the son of Franz Ries, the old friend of the family.

Since his arrival in Vienna Beethoven, again become a pupil, has not been idle. From 1792 to 1796, under Albrechtsberger, he has made a profound study of the fugue — this counterpoint with a human face — and perpetrated a number of "musical skeletons." With Salieri he has studied

the laws of declamation, learned from Förster the art of
quartet-writing, and from Haydn that of composition.

There can be no doubt that such training put to the proof
the self-esteem of this young man whom Haydn laughingly
called his Great Mogul. But could the future author of the
nine symphonies fail to recognize the necessity of thorough
technical study?

So the pupil applies himself assiduously to his masters'
lessons. On the margin of one of his exercises he writes,
"Is this permissible?" and on Salieri's table he traces this
inscription: "The pupil Beethoven passed this way."

Moreover, his tuition comes rather high; he pays his
teachers, and one cannot live for nothing in Vienna.

Hence, he gives lessons to earn his living; at one time he
will lodge in an attic, at another at court.

In fact, he was known at first merely as a virtuoso; thus,
despite his triumphal appearances at Prague, at Pesth, at
Berlin (whence he carried off a gold snuffbox, a present from
the king of Prussia), despite the dread which his prodigious
pianistic talent inspires in his rivals — "He is a demon,"
said Abbé Gelinek, "he will make us all bite the dust!" —
despite all this, chattering, laughing and rattling of cups go
on in the salons where he plays. "The lion has not yet
shaken the bars of his cage." [Von Lenz.]

LUDWIG VAN BEETHOVEN

II

HIS MUSIC

The First Period: Imitation

Although Beethoven, during these first years of serious study under the guidance of good Viennese masters, writes little and is content to prepare at full leisure the issuance of his Opus 1, it must not be supposed that the years spent in Bonn were unproductive. Like Dittersdorf, and Mozart, and nearly all the musicians of that day, Beethoven had begun early to compose — without knowing how. From the Variations which he wrote at the age of twelve on a march by Dressler up to those for four hands (on a theme by Count Waldstein) which immediately precede his Opus 1, he had elaborated numerous compositions. Does the reader care to know the (almost exact) number of pieces written by him during this period of primary study? They total the very respectable figure of *forty-nine*. Among them are three pieces for organ, eleven for harpsichord or piano, seventeen for various instruments or for chamber music, three unfinished concertos, a ballet, two cantatas and thirteen *Lieder*. But whereas, at the present time, many young artists are lost in admiration of their first picture, their first novel, or their first symphony, and cannot rest until these attempts are exhibited or printed or engraved, Beethoven attached no importance whatever to the creations of those ten years. Aside from the three piano-sonatas, the first Variations and a song, which were written for a musical magazine (Speeler's "Blumenlese") in 1782–83, and published therein, he did not wish at that time to have any of these attempts engraved;

[13]

while we shall find certain of these "sins of youth" bearing opus-numbers, that is because they served him, much later, for calming the impatience of exigent publishers.*

Beethoven, therefore, had finished these complementary studies when he decided to write "Opus 1" on the manuscript of the three trios ordered by Prince Lichnowsky and so painfully perfected in the course of 1793 and 1794. In point of fact, it is from this twenty-third year of his life that we may date his definitive entrance on the career of a composer. The period with which we are occupied at present, extending from 1793 to 1801, comprises about eighty works: Twenty sonatas for piano, or violin, or violoncello, or horn; eight trios for piano and strings; six string-quartets; a score of pieces for piano with various instruments; two collections of Viennese dances; music to the ballet *Prometheus;* twelve songs; three piano-concertos; the grand Septet; and the First Symphony.

The naming of the first period "the period of imitation" can be justified without difficulty; for we constantly meet with traces of a mind preoccupied with, or unconsciously copying, some work of his contemporaries or of the preceding generation. Having only a slight, or incomplete, acquaintance with the grand ancestral figures of music, Beethoven does not yet employ that polyphonic style which is later to present us the last quartets; though familiar with Bach's pieces for harpsichord, he does not venture on writing in the fugued style exhibited in his third period. A virtuoso by vocation, he intends to remain a virtuoso, and almost all

* While Beethoven was alive, twenty-one of these works were issued at various dates; his brother Carl sold some others for his own profit; twenty-eight remained unpublished.

TITLE PAGE OF BEETHOVEN'S FIRST PRINTED COMPOSITIONS

Published when he was eleven years of age, and dedicated to Maximilian Friedrich,
Archbishop and Elector of Cologne

that flows from his pen conforms to the conventions of musicians of that day with respect to virtuosi.

Indeed, he was launched on his artistic career, as we have seen, as a pianist and improvisor; his talent on the harpsichord was renowned; his teacher Neefe considered him one of the most skilled pianists of Germany. Hence, ever since arriving in Vienna, his prodigality of concerts public and private.

On the 29th and 30th of November, 1795, he played at the Charity Concerts organized by Haydn for the benefit of the widows of victims of the war; on January the 8th, 1796, he played at the concert given by the singer Maria Bolla, under Haydn's conductorship; on a tour through Germany he improvised before the court at Berlin, and allied himself with Prince Ludwig of Prussia; in 1797 he played at a concert given in Vienna by the Romberg brothers, and at Schuppanzigh's concert; on April the 2d, 1798, he played at a concert before the Imperial Court, and competed in execution and improvisation with the pianist Woelffl — famous then, quite forgotten now. Is it surprising that his first compositions should be modified by this manner of living, and that he should have sought, during this period, after external and conventional effect rather than the expression of his own genius?

However this may be, there were three musicians whose influence then made itself felt in Beethoven's works: C. Ph. Em. Bach, Fr. Wilhelm Rust, and, above all, Joseph Haydn.

His character as a man of the north in no way predisposed him, like Mozart, for example, to let himself be overmastered by the facile charm of Italian melody, and in his piano-pieces nothing reminds one of the style of foreign masters;

one meets neither Couperin's ornamental manner nor the original style of D. Scarlatti. No; one feels that he was under the spell of his immediate artistic ancestry, of the Germans who were so nearly his contemporaries.

Beethoven was eighteen when C. Ph. E. Bach died at Hamburg, and it was from the didactic works of the son of Johann Sebastian that he obtained his knowledge of pianistic art. Concurrently with the "Well-tempered Clavichord" Neefe made the young man acquainted with the two sets of six sonatas for cembalo, dedicated to the kings of Prussia and Württemberg respectively, which were then widely known and which had revealed *modern* music to Haydn himself. This same Neefe, who had connections in Dessau, whither he returned to die, could not fail to know the works of Fr. W. Rust, and (though explicit documentary evidence on this head is lacking) it is altogether probable that he had his pupil practise at least the first six sonatas by the Kapell-meister to the Prince of Anhalt, engraved in Leipzig 1775–1778, when Neefe was conductor of orchestra in that town.

As to Haydn's influence, that is no matter for surprise; for, consciously or not, every diligent pupil always borrows, at the outset, his master's processes.

This is the proper place — as a matter of simple justice — to rectify a wholly erroneous opinion which, founded on a misunderstanding, has been handed on by a certain number of historiographers, and influenced even von Lenz himself. We refer to Haydn's supposed jealousy of his pupil, which is said to have moved him to leave uncorrected mistakes in the latter's exercises. From this it is but a step to affirm that Haydn taught Beethoven nothing, and to conclude that Beethoven was *self-taught*. The critics above referred to

[16]

have hastened to take this step, apparently without imagining that in so doing they were guilty, not only of inaccuracy, but of calumny.

To suppose the aged Haydn, then in the zenith of his fame, capable of such meanness, of such an abuse of confidence in relation to his youthful disciple, is to misjudge his character entirely and to set it in opposition to the actions of his whole life.

From the fact that Haydn failed to correct mistakes in the contrapuntal exercises,* it does not in the least follow that he was not a conscientious and perspicacious tutor for the young man recommended to him by the Archbishop-Elector. We must not forget that Haydn was teaching Beethoven *composition;* now, while the study of counterpoint is necessary for the acquisition of fluency and correctness in writing, it is quite different from that of composition, which supposes the student to have emerged from the difficulties of preliminary training. The rôle of a teacher of composition is not to correct faults of orthography; he has something radically different to do with his pupil's mind!

In all that concerned these studies in fluency, as one might call them, from simple counterpoint up to the Chinese puzzles of double-chorus and double-fugue, Albrechtsberger took charge of the youthful Beethoven's instruction; but what the latter learned from the lessons and fruitful conversation with Haydn was otherwise profitable and precious for the future author of the Mass in *D*. "Papa Haydn" taught him to discriminate, to dispose his musical elements in logical fashion — in a word, to construct, which is the whole

* See Haydn's corrections in the interesting volume by Nottebohm, "Beethoven's Studien" (Leipzig, 1873).

art of the composer; and so Beethoven, whatever Ries —
always to be accepted cautiously — may say to the contrary,
remained profoundly grateful to his master; a thousand
details might be cited to prove it. Nothing, not even the
salutary advice which Haydn gave his pupil with regard to
the first three Trios, but has been travestied and proffered
as a proof of jealousy or incomprehension. Flagrant in-
justice, of a truth! for Haydn had the best of reasons for
advising Beethoven to revise his first trios, which were over-
laden with details and ill-balanced in their primitive version,
more especially the third in *C* minor, then subjected to a
complete recasting. The writer of the trios himself abundantly recognized the services rendered him by the master in
this particular; a long time after, while chatting with Drouet,
the flute-player, he observed, "These trios were not engraved
in the form in which I first wrote them. On rereading my
manuscripts I asked myself if I had not been foolish to bring
together in a single piece enough material for twenty. . . . .
At the beginning I should have perpetrated the wildest
absurdities, had it not been for the good advice of Papa
Haydn and Albrechtsberger."

We are safe, therefore, in asserting that Haydn was, for
Beethoven, a valued guide whose counsels, imparted while
they were out walking, or during the long conversations held
at the café where the pupil treated the master to a cup of
chocolate (twenty-two *Kreutzer* for the two cups), opened
the young man's mind to the great problems of composition,
of the key-scheme and musical architecture.

Let us now return to the influences betrayed by the first
manner of the master of Bonn.

Of this first Beethoven one might say that he borrows from

Ph. E. Bach his *style* of piano-writing, of W. Rust his creative *thought, and of Haydn his impeccable architecture*.

The imitation of Em. Bach's style is especially striking in his earliest works. The Largo of the second trio (Opus 1) exhibits a distribution of light and shade, and of the accents, similar to that which Frederick the Great's musician was accustomed to employ; the sonatas, and particularly the first, in *F* minor, remind one of the "Prussian" sonatas even thematically; the Finale bears very close kinship to the third sonata (Book 3) of the collection "for connoisseurs and amateurs," although more refined. And in numerous other pieces, notably Op. 10, No. 2, such imitation can be discovered.

Turning to Rust's works, do we not recognize his mode of thought, and even of expressing his thought, in Beethoven's second sonata for piano? And finally, to be brief, did not the same poetic sentiment dictate the last movement of Beethoven's sixth quartet (1799) and the Finale of the eighth sonata by the Dessau composer? This *Malinconia* interrupted by the exposition of a joyous rondo, to reappear amidst rustic merrymaking — is it not moulded, so to speak (at least in its form), on the *Schwermuth* (melancholy) of Rust followed, by way of completion and consolation, by a joyous theme (*Frohsinn*) of a wholly pastoral mood, almost Beethoven-like?

As far as Haydn is concerned, the imitation is rather in form than in substance. One might say that the pupil, not quite sure that he can walk alone, has borrowed his master's gold-knobbed cane, yet without going so far as to put on the fine buckle-shoes of the Father of the Symphony. Many characteristics peculiar to Haydn's manner of construction are again met with in Beethoven's youthful works. It was from the sonatas and quartets of Haydn's last period that Beethoven took this formation of the *second theme* out of three elements, in three phrases which, though distinct, are inseparable one from the other.

This formation does not commonly occur with either Mozart or Clementi, or with their contemporaries; but it is already observable, although in a rudimentary form, in Em. Bach's "Württemberg" sonatas, whereof Haydn was the true continuator.

Like Haydn, our young Beethoven loves "piquant" episodes, short excursions into keys distant from the ruling tonality; even the unusual rhythms and displacements of accent so habitual with Beethoven are employed in the same way by the maestro of the princes Esterhazy. And if the Scherzo of the first string-quartet (Op. 18) seems so original in cast by reason of its rhythm, which constitutes a series of measures whose time-signatures might be written 3–3–2, do we not notice with astonishment, in Haydn's Farewell Symphony, a minuet no less curious, whose periodic rhythm is established by 4, 2, 3 and 3 measures?

Following his teacher's lead, Beethoven is fond of treating the same musical theme several times in various ways, as in the Minuet of the Septet (Op. 20) and the Rondo of Op. 49, No. 2; later, in the *Air de ballet* of *Prometheus* repeated in the Variations, and becoming the Finale of the Third Symphony.

Still better, in his sonata for piano Op. 10, No. 2, he uses one of Haydn's own themes (that of the sonata which bears, in most editions, the number 58), and is so taken with this melody that he employs it, with insignificant alterations, in

G. S. NEEFE
1748–1798

(Gesellschaft der Musikfreunde,
Vienna)

J. G. ALBRECHTSBERGER
1736–1800

(Historical Museum at Frankfort-
on-the-Main)

F. J. HAYDN
1732–1800

(By Mansfeld)

THE THREE TEACHERS OF BEETHOVEN

a certain number of his later compositions, down to the sonata Op. 110, in 1821.

It would be useless to enumerate here all of Beethoven's works in which these three influences show themselves, even when the master is in the full flower of his genius. Let it suffice to note the sonata Op. 57, whose four wearisome tones db–db–db–c are already to be found in Haydn's sonata to Frau Genziger, and in Rust's sonata in $F\sharp$ minor; a theme in the Württemberg sonata in $A\flat$ major by Em. Bach is identically the same as that of the Finale of the sonata Op. 27, No. 2 (the "Moonlight Sonata"); and finally, the Adagio of the sonata for violin and lute, by Rust, bears an astounding resemblance to the melody of the superb Andante which forms the middle movement of the trio Op. 97, dedicated to Archduke Rudolph.

From all the preceding it is not rash to conclude that this portion of Beethoven's career was a period of *imitation;* — in no way servile, be it understood, for in the majority of the important works a keen-sighted observer can trace the characteristics which were afterwards to grow into the genial originality of Beethoven. True enough, these flights are as yet not very bold, and give but a faint idea of the towering heights attained in the second and, above all, the third period.

Before ending this chapter we should mention with greater detail some few works which won immediate success, or which formed sketches for grand conceptions of later date.

(1) **Adelaide.** Song on a text by Matthison, composed in 1796, published in 1797. Curiously enough, this worklet, a romance neither better nor worse than most of the innumerable romances of that epoch, contributed powerfully to the

renommée of Beethoven, whose serious compositions were long to remain almost unknown. Did the young pupil of Neefe give this text a musical setting when influenced by a thought or memory of some little love-affair adumbrated beneath the hospitable roof of the Breunings? Was she, who inspired this melody, Jeannette von Honrath? Was she Wilhelmine von Westerholdt? The point is difficult to decide. But this *Adelaide* soon passed for the dolorous cry of a wounded heart, for the supreme plaint of the wretched lover, calling to his beloved even amid the shades of the tomb. The vogue of this romance was such that in a very short time it was published under *fifty-two* different forms! — twenty-eight with *pianoforte*, eleven with guitar, etc.; besides twenty-one transcriptions for divers instruments, *sixteen of them being for piano, four hands!*

And nevertheless, there is no difficulty whatever in considering this piece as one of Beethoven's poorest productions — he was never a great writer of *Lieder*. There is nothing really expressive in it; it is just one more romance — that is all. And it is equally a new proof of the ancient verity that, in all times, the public reserves its favors for mediocre works, passing by genuine beauty with indifference.

(2) **The Pathetic Sonata,** Opus 13 (1798). Another active agent of success, both at the time when this work appeared and, in the sequel, down to the third quarter of the nineteenth century!* The same rôle devolved upon the Septet for clarinet, bassoon, horn, violin, viola, violoncello and bass.

* See the amusing fantasy by von Lenz on the rôle played by this sonata in boarding-schools "and other institutions where one does *not* learn to play the piano." ("Beethoven et ses trois styles.")

The interest of the Pathetic Sonata resides, not so much in the music itself, as in its architecture, rather peculiar and rare at that epoch. A cyclic motive of four notes, *g, c, d, e♭*, proceeds to the formation of the three movements of the work. This motive, buttressed by other themes, enters into a conflict from the first movement onward with the figure displayed in the introduction, which latter, losing a member at each episode of the struggle, ends by owning itself defeated. In the Finale the victorious motive (which, says von Lenz, one should "exalt to pathetic expression") reappears merrily to form the refrain of the rondo.

We cite this sonata, not because it offers a greater aggregate of beauty than its congeners of the first period, but as forming the point of departure for that "struggle between two principles" whose vital necessity in all tonal constructions was already affirmed by Beethoven, and employed by him with far more confidence in a number of subsequent works.

(3) **Seufzer eines Ungeliebten** (The Sigh of One Unloved), *Lied* on words by Bürger (1796). The melody itself would be in no wise more interesting than that of *Adelaide*, mentioned above, were not the theme which forms the subject of the second part — called *Gegenliebe* (Mutual Love) — precisely the one which Beethoven again employed in his *Fantasie* for piano, orchestra and chorus in 1808, and which, in itself, is nothing more nor less than a sketch — rather primitive, to be sure, but, for that very reason, curious — of the Finale of the Ninth Symphony. Thus, during well-nigh thirty years, this theme haunted Beethoven's soul; and throughout, as we shall see, he attaches to it this same signification of mutual love.

On bringing this period to a close, it is of interest to observe how far Beethoven, while he yet lisps, pushes his scrupulous conscientiousness in art. In 1794 he received from Count Apponyi an order for three string-quartets. The string-quartet, it must be said, is one of the most difficult forms of composition, and requires full maturity of mind and talent. From the following year on the young man strives to discharge his obligation towards his noble patron; twice he attempts a realization of this difficult style of composition — a quartet of well-balanced sonority. He does not succeed — and has the honesty to admit it. Not until four years thereafter does he decide to write the six Lobkowitz quartets, certain constructions in which recall those employed by K. Stamitz, Cannabich, and other musicians of the second rank belonging to the Mannheim school. "Only from to-day onward," declares Beethoven to a friend, "do I begin to know how to write a quartet."

With regard to the symphony he exercised equal reserve. Though familiar through early study with the art of instrumentation, it was only after long delay that he approached the composition of a symphony; and yet this first attempt, despite the amazement or the protestations of his contemporaries concerning the "strangeness" of the first measure, can in truth be viewed by us as merely an adroit imitation of Haydn's last works of this kind.*

And now let us leave Beethoven, the pupil of genius, (but who, for all that, is as yet a "good pupil,") to welcome upon

---

* It is to this First Period that we must relegate the unpublished symphony about which the University of Jena has been making such a pother, and whose genuineness has by no means been demonstrated.

BEETHOVEN, AGED TWENTY-SIX (1796)

Design by G. Stainhauser; engraving by J. Neidl, executed for the
publisher Artaria

the scene, with the year 1801, a different and entirely recon-
stituted Beethoven.

How was this transformation achieved?   To what causes
can we attribute it?   These are questions to be taken up in
the musical part of the following chapter.

THE SECOND PERIOD

FROM 1801 TO 1815

III

HIS LIFE

THE generosity displayed towards the youthful Beethoven by the noblemen of Vienna, has received no adequate recognition. The Lichnowsky family alone subscribed for thirty-two copies of the trios, Op. 1. Prince Carl presided at the rehearsals of new works. The story goes that at the interminable rehearsal of *Christ on the Mount of Olives* the prince had lavish distribution made of refreshments, all sorts of cold meats, etc., to the members of orchestra and chorus, in order to restrain their impatience. — It was a serious matter when *Fidelio* was taken in hand; there was a conspiracy to make cuts. The princess, seated at the piano, indicated the passages to be sacrificed and sought to pacify Beethoven, who, red with rage, refused to give up this aria, clung to that, and all in despite of the good intentions of friends who desired, before everything else, the success of the opera.

What with the regular Wednesday matinées at the Prince's, the theatrical garden parties of Dr. Franck, the quartet evenings on Sundays and Thursdays at the home of either Zizius or Förster, and the usual soirées of Baron van Swieten, Beethoven was continually active. At the house of Count Rasoumowsky (who had married the second of the "three

Graces," the sister of Princess Lichnowsky) he found young
and ardent interpreters who were always ready to try his
works "hot, as if just out of the oven"; and he liked to
gather the remarks of his professional brethren. Such were
the burly Schuppanzigh; the viola-player Weiss, tall and
thin; Lincke, the lame violoncellist, and his temporary
amateur substitute, the famous *Musikbaron* Zmeskall von
Domanowecz, a stiff little man with very thick white hair
and of jovial habit, who will serve as a butt for innumerable
puns — Beethoven's innocent passion.

All in all, it will be seen that the legend of the "unappre-
ciated Beethoven" rests on slender foundations.

Let us seek out the musician in a companionship yet nearer
to his heart — that of his pupils in piano-playing. Let us
linger for a moment at the home of Countess Deym (*née* von
Brunswick), the lovely Pepi, younger sister of the melancholy
Theresa. At the age of twenty-four this latter is an *intel-
lectuelle*, a trifle malformed, but so literary and distinguished!
Both have requested lessons of the young and celebrated
virtuoso. Their brother Franz, a violoncellist and fanatical
melomaniac, will soon become his intimate friend, and the
lindens of the château of Márton Vásár, each one of which
bore the name of a friend, will more than once greet the
visitor Beethoven.

What a delightful gathering of young girls and young
wives was there! And how they flock after Herr van Beethoven, each trying to pluck his sleeve and induce him to
inscribe a few notes in an album. In requital whereof he
will gallantly insist that his suppliants' pretty fingers shall
embroider him a handkerchief or a collar. In the midst of
this parterre, resplendent as a rare flower, is Giulietta Guic-

ciardi, his future pupil. A daughter of the house of Brunswick, this little provincial, just arrived from Trieste, is
possibly the least gifted of the gathering, but so seductive
with the wiles of Southern coquetry! . . . And Beethoven
is smitten, and has dreams; aided by the prefix "van," may
he not aspire to the young patrician's hand? Did she listen
to him? We have no proof of it except that letter about
"the enchanting child who loves me, and whom I love,"
wherein the artist unveils his secret to a friend. No further
mention is made of it, however, the parents being naturally
opposed to such a mésalliance. Giulietta became Countess
of Gallenberg.

But Beethoven's wound was grievous. Twenty years
later, telling Schindler about the reverses of fortune which
had overtaken the Gallenbergs and the visit paid him by the
inconsistent Giulietta in connection with them, he repeated
fondly, "How lovely she still was!" How can we withhold
our deep commiseration on reading, in a letter written on
the eve of his rival's nuptials (November the 2d, 1803), this
cry of suppressed anguish: "Ah! what terrible moments
there are in life — and yet we must accept them."

For the musician this spiritual trial was the more cruel
because it came in addition to the menace of a dreadful
physical affliction. Since 1796, Beethoven felt that he was
growing deaf. He hardly dared speak of it to his friends
Wegeler and Amenda. "How confess the weakness of a
sense which I should possess in fuller perfection than any
other?" He had hastened from specialist to specialist.
Vering, Franck, Schmidt, Bertolini, Father Weiss, had in
turn recommended cold baths, hot baths, vesicatories, gal-
vanism, injections of oil or of tea. . . . Nothing helped.

Soon he will give over his last hope. "There is no use in hiding it; everybody knows it; even the players have noticed it." And thenceforward he will not appear without his ear-trumpet.

Just now he feels his wretchedness and isolation more keenly. He withdraws to Heiligenstadt; he wishes to die; he writes that dolorous and romantic "will" quoted somewhat too often: "As the leaves of autumn fall and wither, thus — thus have withered my hopes!" Do we not seem to behold him in the attitude imagined by the painter Mähler — unhappy of mien, his left hand resting on a lyre, his right sketching a rhythm, in the background a temple to Apollo?

Poor Beethoven! How much of suffering is yet in store for him before he becomes the "philosopher" he thinks himself to be! And then, can a man look on, unmoved, while his country is torn asunder? There is a sound of trumpets, of hostile assault; troops press forward and cannon thunder through the valley of the Danube. The French invaders are still here; and in the wineroom of an evening with his friends Breuning and Gleichenstein, both employed at the Ministry of War, nothing is talked of but manœuvres and battles, Arcola, Hochstädt, Hohenlinden. Beethoven's ardent hatred of these invaders finds vent in bitter sallies against these "Gallo-Franks, deaf to the appeal of goodness and truth, inapt for any reasonable policy." Nevertheless, Bernadotte, an assiduous guest at the Austrian Court, where he is already in training for his future kingship; Bernadotte, the new ambassador to whom Kreutzer presented him, has received him cordially. After the musical sessions at the embassy, Beethoven hears tales of the Egyptian campaign, of Bonaparte's feats of genius. How can he help admiring this great man, the living personification of his beloved Greek and Roman heroes? And amid this stirring epic atmosphere the Third Symphony leaps from his brain.

But amidst the happenings of daily life Beethoven has never ceased to dream of marriage and tranquil conjugal happiness. This he proves by choosing for the book of his opera something quite different from the German fairy-plays proposed by others, the rather simple scenario by the excellent Bouilly entitled *Fidelio, or Conjugal Love*, already set to music by Gaveau and Paër. Florestan, the object of conjugal devotion, who so fitly impersonated the sentiments of our honest Beethoven; — Florestan, the poor prisoner persecuted by a wicked warden and restored to freedom by a good magistrate; — Florestan has nothing in common, we must admit, with those uninteresting inmates of the Bastille to whom he has been likened; but his woes were of a sort to move a people yet thrilled by a memory of the jails of the Terror* and, in particular, of the long agony endured in the prison of the Temple by the daughter of Maria Theresa. *Fidelio* appeared on the bills at the moment when Austerlitz had opened the gates of the capital to Napoleon; the audience was composed solely of officers of the victorious army, and the pecuniary success was null.

Fortunately for Beethoven, faithful friends watched over him. Between him and Breuning, whose lodgings hard by

* In Vol. II of "Mes Récapitulations," p. 81, Bouilly, the administrator of the Department of Indre-et-Loire during the Terror, declares that he desired to celebrate, in his piece, "the heroism and devotion of one of the ladies of Touraine whose generous endeavors I had the privilege of seconding." Other operas à la mode, Cherubini's *Water-Carrier*, for instance, treated the same subject.

the ramparts he shared, occasion for dissension was, however, not lacking, because of their daily relations. They quarrelled, but were reconciled directly:- "Beneath this portrait, my dear, my good Stephen, may all that has so long stood between us be buried forever!" Besides, could one harbor resentment for the good Beethoven? Breuning occupied his nights in arranging the libretto for *Fidelio,* and, aided by Beethoven's brothers, sought to gain a clear insight into the financial side of the matter, for at this date the young composer already had but one embarrassment, that of selecting his publisher. "They will pay me the price that I shall ask," he writes; "what happiness, to be able to help friends in distress!"

Another friendship, feminine this time, supervened to console him for the deceptions of love. Its incarnation was a woman of twenty-five, pretty and delicate, surrounded by three charming children, "Fritzi the unique, and the two Marias." Since years half-paralyzed, keenly alive to naught beside music, Countess Erdödy was transfigured when able to drag herself as far as the piano. Beethoven had permission to come when he pleased to the home of the grand Hungarian dame, and the latter had erected in his honor, beneath the magnificent shade-trees of Jedlersee, a rustic temple whence were sent messages in verse "to the first-born of Apollo, his laurel-crowned Majesty, etc." She was his confidante — "his confessor," as he will say later. She was to become his adviser.

To her Vienna owes it, that Beethoven remained there.

Just then a series of misadventures rained upon the poor embittered musician, irritated without cause, prone to see cabals on every side. A concert from which he expected great things (December 22d, 1808) because of his production thereat of two new wonder-works, the Symphony in *C* minor and the Pastoral, nearly occasioned his departure. In his ardor of gesticulation as conductor he knocked down the candles at his desk and nearly put out one of the orchestra-helper's eyes, to the great delight of the audience. The prima donna missed her cues because, some days previously, he had treated her fiancé "like a blockhead;" the second lady was vexed because she had been chosen as a mere stop-gap; a third lost her head and stammered through her part. In the concert-hall the people were shivering with cold. To cap the climax, a missed repeat in the Fantasia with chorus threw the whole orchestra off the track and caused the precipitate flight of the audience, when Beethoven, in tones of thunder, demanded a *da capo*.

After this, he felt that the Viennese deserved a lesson. And at this juncture a splendid position is offered him: "600 ducats in gold, only a few concerts to prepare, an orchestra at my disposition, with plenty of leisure to compose great works." His mouth waters at the prospect.

However, it is the new king of Westphalia, Jérome Bonaparte, who thus invites him to his court.

Countess Erdödy has learned the news. In the twinkling of an eye she gathers all her friends around her to consider taking measures to prevent such a scandal — their Beethoven forced to expatriate himself! But while the affair is being arranged, care has to be taken not to alarm the susceptibilities of the great man, and to leave him a hope of obtaining some official position in Austria, "his dearest wish," in view of his matrimonial establishment.

By mutual understanding the three princes Rudolph,

BEETHOVEN'S NEW YEAR'S GREETING TO
BARONESS DOROTHEA ERTMANN (1804)

LUDWIG VAN BEETHOVEN

Kinsky and Lobkowitz signed the agreement of March the 1st, 1809, which assured to Beethoven an annual income of four thousand florins. Beethoven will not go "to enjoy the ham of Westphalia"; on this he congratulates himself, with good reason, in a letter to his friend Gleichenstein. Indeed, what would have become of him, the outspoken antisemite, in the midst of the gilded ghetto which was then the Court of Cassel, this scene wherein looseness of morals vied with wasteful finance? Our question is answered by Baron de Trémont, a French visitor who has left us one of the most vivid descriptions extant concerning the great musician's private life:* "He would not have stayed there six months." — Less than a year thereafter the orgy of fraud had reached such a pitch that the court officials were left unpaid.

Was it not better to suffer at home with the rest?

Though Beethoven lived through the days of anguish preceding the bombardment of Vienna, though cannon-shots broke his heart and shattered his eardrums, though at the fight of Wagram ("inter lacrymas et luctum") his beloved banks of the Danube, his Prater and his ramparts, lay before him devastated and disfigured by the activities of warfare, though he was deprived (in 1809) of his "indispensable summer vacation" and his long and fruitful excursions on the slopes of the Kahlenberg, he at least had the satisfaction of giving free utterance to his patriotic faith in the music to *Egmont*, in the military marches dedicated to Archduke Anthony, and of celebrating, by his admirable Sonata Op.

* *Cf.* Baron de Trémont's narrative in the "Guide musical" for March, 1892. M. Michel Brenet brought this manuscript to light at the National Library ten years prior to its so-called "discovery" as communicated to the review "Die Musik" in 1902.

81, the return of Archduke Rudolph to the capital — a presage of "golden peace."

For the rest, and despite the terrible war-taxes which burden his budget, the Master seems to find new zest in life. He assumes an amiable mien; he actually orders himself a suit of clothes, a hat, a fine cambric shirt — a complete trousseau. He reappears "newly apparelled" on the Prater or in the fashionable cabaret "Zum wilden Mann." He has a household staff, a servant in livery. And if Wegeler is surprised that he should demand, *dare dare*, a copy of his birth-certificate, Zmeskall is none the less so on finding himself commissioned by Beethoven to purchase a looking-glass!

For whom all these expenditures? They date from his reception, in attendance on his friend Baron Gleichenstein, into a charming home enlivened by the laughter of two young girls, Theresa and Anna Malfatti; the latter soon to be betrothed to the Baron. As for Theresa, a living ray of sunshine, a brunette of medallion-like profile, she lightly leaps from subject to subject "and treats everything in life with such levity" that Beethoven reproaches her with it while feeling his heart, that so craves joy, moved to the core by that "divine gayety." Ah! could he only please — this time! He caresses doggy "Gigons" and takes him out walking; he writes long letters that are almost declarations, and wherein he calls forests, trees, rocks, to witness: "Ye, at least, return the echo that man expects of you!" — But, alas! Theresa too desired to become a baroness, and when Beethoven divulges to his friend his hope of being accepted, the sky falls about his ears. Another disillusionment! — bitter reproaches to the fiancé of Anna, who is no whit to blame; the eternal plaint of one discarded: "For thee, poor Beethoven, no happiness may be expected outside thyself. Thou wilt have to create everything within. Only in the ideal world shalt thou find her who loves thee!" Is not this already a presage of his third period? Now he is again whelmed in gloom, more and more obsessed by the deafness closing around him with an ever-thickening wall.

So much the more sympathetic for others' woes, he endeavors to divert the daughter of the illustrious Birkenstock with his music. She had married a Brentano of Frankfort, and had been ill ever since her marriage. Like Mme. von Erdödy, she was surrounded by beautiful children; and Beethoven, who adored children (remember his delightful letter to little Emilie von H.), brought them bonbons, composed a little trio for Maximilienne, and promised her a grand sonata for later. The house was filled with objects of art and curiosities; Beethoven improvised to the sound of the flowing Danube floating in through the open window with the fragrance of the lindens. One day when he was at the piano, two hands were placed on his shoulders and a voice close to his ear cried, "My name is Brentano!" From this characteristic action we instantly recognize the celebrated Bettina, Franz's younger sister, "so small at twenty-two that she appeared to be twelve or thirteen."

How should the inflammable Beethoven resist this imp whose walk was a dance, and who vaults on to his knees with the same assurance with which she climbed into Goethe's lap, or to the rosette in the cathedral at Cologne? How well she understands the art of flattery and adulation! "You are ravishing, my youthful dancer," Goethe told her; "at each step you cast us a crown." Alas! 'tis true, if Bettina is enchanted with Beethoven's music, she is none the less so with Durante's; if she loves Goethe, she also loves the French hussars and the handsome Turks in the Prater, whose slippers she twirls at the end of a stick for her amusement. For the rest, "where folly ends with other people, it begins with the Brentanos."

Where Bettina deserves honor, as Sainte-Beuve very rightly remarks, is in her playing the dual rôle of interpreter between Goethe and Beethoven. They were "two Magi whose distant greetings were borne by this little elfin page who so aptly conveyed the messages." Beethoven's interview with the Jupiter Olympus of Weimar occurred by the springs of Teplitz in July, 1812; it passed as might be expected from the respectful admiration which the musician always expressed for the author of "Faust." What did these two great men say to each other? What could Beethoven hear, with his poor closed ears? Did the proud Goethe deign to inscribe his marvelous words on the pitiable conversation-tablets? Our sole witness is a few letters from Beethoven to Bettina.

But can one really put faith in the testimony of this charming victim of hallucination? Must we recall, in this connection, that famous letter whereof no one has ever seen the original, in which Beethoven is represented on the promenade confronted with the imperial family, his hat pulled down over his eyes, his overcoat buttoned, pushing with folded arms through their very midst, while Goethe, hat in hand, steps aside with a profound obeisance?

"Duke Rudolph lifted his hat to me, the empress saluted me first." The anecdote, it must be confessed, does greater credit to the delicacy of the Austrian princes' feelings than

to Beethoven's good manners. But we may be permitted
a few observations: If the Countess von Arnim was at that
time in Teplitz, as the visitors' list proves, why did Beethoven
write to her? Why did he ostentatiously apply the title of
"Duke" to the man whom he otherwise invariably calls his
"dear Archduke?" And why, finally, does Bettina tell the
story quite differently in her letter to Pückler-Muskau?
Truly, a questionable case! — Let us once more conclude
that one should view with strong suspicion the words and
writings of the youthful Bettina.

At Teplitz Beethoven likewise joined a group of interesting patriots and literary folk who, at the sign of the Star (an
hotel frequented by people of fashion), held reunions under
the sceptre of Countess von der Recke. Polished gentlemen, young officers, engaging ladies — what a rare find,
could they but lay hands on the author of the music to
Egmont! And one fine day this miracle was achieved by the
lovely eyes of Rachel Levin, "the image of other cherished
features."

Beethoven, who till then had persisted in dining alone,
consented to take part in the gatherings of the society. Here
his heart will be fettered anew, this time by Amalie Sebald,
the beautiful and virtuous Berlin singer. In her praise he
will indite the doggerel verse:

> Ludwig van Beethoven
> den Sie, wenn Sie auch wollten,
> doch nicht vergessen sollten.*

> * Ludwig van Beethoven:
> Howe'er you might endeavor,
> You should forget him never.

When he is taken ill, the lovely Amalie acts as his nurse; she supervises his dietary, forbids his morning promenades in the autumnal mists, she calls him "my dear tyrant"; he addresses her as "Amalie," and to his lips there mount ardent avowals which he will never dare utter. — "Five years ago," he afterwards declared to Giannatasio del Rio, "I found the woman of my dreams, but I could not make up my mind to go further." Did he feel a presentiment that his advances would not be well received? Did he shrink in dread of refusal by an artist, in view of former experiences with a noblewoman and a *bourgeoise?*

Were you, kind Amalie Sebald, that "immortal beloved" of whom so much has been said? — Beethoven, who "always had a love-affair on his hands," might well thus have apostrophized ye in turn: — You, seductive Giulietta; you, brilliant Gherardi; you, Countess Babette, the homely beauty to whom were dedicated the Variations Opus 34, and the first Piano-Concerto; you, the two Theresas, one frivolous, one serious; you, "dear Cecilie Dorothea"; you, Lady of the Jeglersee; you, charming Marie Bigot of France, who read for the first time, in the manuscript of the Appassionata drenched by the tempest, those immortal pages; you, Marie Pachler-Koschak, the "goddess of Graz," an autumnal passion whom the master constituted "the true guardian of the offspring of his spirit"; you, impish Bettina; and lastly you, the Unknown of 1816 for whose smile he lay in wait: "When M. went by just now, I thought she looked at me;" — through his music he loved ye all. Had ye not found yourselves in the path of a great man, posterity would doubtless have known nothing of you, nor would ye have disputed the honor of having inspired the pencilled lines, half-effaced, "My Angel, my All, my Self. . . ." Music alone may claim this honor as her very own. Did ye for a while illumine his pathway, ye brought him suffering, as well: "He who sows love," wrote Beethoven, "reaps tears." Yet it is through these tears that we are possessed of the inward Beethoven, the grand Beethoven of the third period.

The treatment at Teplitz restored the invalid to health and good humor for some days. Despite the disordered state of his finances (the payment of his annuity had just been interrupted by the legal advisers of the too-magnificent Lobkowitz, and as a result of Kinsky's accidental death*); despite the difficulty of transacting business with publishers involved in the consequences of the Continental System, and who sent him translations of Tacitus and Euripides in lieu of cash, Beethoven forgets his own evil plight to think of others. Either it is his poor Breuning, now a widower, on whom he showers tender attentions; or it is his dying brother Carl whose whims he would gratify; or his other brother, the druggist, whom he endeavors to rescue from the toils of his mistress, a former servant. To-day he organizes a charity concert for victims of the Baden disaster; tomorrow he sends bundles of his music for an "Academie" (concert) for the benefit of the Ursulines at Graz, demanding in exchange only the "prayers of holy women and their pupils."

Nevertheless, Frau Streicher finds him wholly destitute, in rags. "The condition of my footwear," he laughingly declares, "keeps me at home perforce." Just then, to help

---

* The official inventory of Beethoven's effects, and the account-books of the Kinsky family, prove that since 1815 the three annuities were paid very regularly, for all that has been said to the contrary.

him replenish his purse, Maelzel, the Viennese Vaucanson,* who had long sought an undiscoverable ear-trumpet to suit Beethoven's needs, made him the following offer: To produce the music of two new symphonies in combination with an exhibition of a certain automatic trumpet which should execute the military signals of the Grande Armée; Maelzel answering for the enthusiasm of the Viennese public.

The event proved him right. The benefit concerts on December 8th and 12th, 1813, for the wounded at the battle of Hanau, attracted more than three thousand auditors. In a resounding proclamation "alla Bonaparte" Beethoven — who had gathered under his bâton all that Austria then numbered among her illustrious musicians, Hummel, Spohr, Mayseder, Salieri, Meyerbeer (who, charged with the part of the bass drum, missed his entry) — thanked his troops "for having laid upon the altar of their country the fruit of their talents."

Strange irony of fate! The *Battle of Vittoria*, that mediocre pot-pourri of the airs of *Marlborough*, *Rule Britannia*, and *God save the King*, for which Beethoven himself said "he would not give two-pence," was to do more for his success than all his symphonies!

At the Congress of Vienna, in 1814, the Archduke presented his Master to all the crowned heads. And now not merely "great ladies," but queens and empresses, overwhelm him with gifts and compliments. He becomes popular. His music figures on the programs of all the student societies, of all the military bands; peasants from the Kahlenberg, recognizing him, offer him cherries on coming out after the

* Jacques de V., a mechanician and maker of celebrated automatons.

production of the Seventh Symphony. His *Fidelio* is revived; he almost arrives at a realization of his dream — the
direction of the imperial Kapelle; he has reached the apogee
of his glory: "Just write my address 'Beethoven, Vienna;'
that is enough," he writes to Amenda. But all the while
"he finds himself more lonely than ever in the great city,"
and he has forebodings:

"Your Highness wishes that I should be with you, and
Art claims me no less; one day I am at Schönbrunn, the
next here. Every day I receive new orders from abroad.
But, even from the standpoint of art, I cannot help feeling a
certain anxiety in view of this undeserved fame. Happiness
pursues me, therefore, I tremble lest some new calamity
confront me!"

IV

HIS MUSIC

SECOND PERIOD: TRANSITION

WHOEVER attempts to make out a chronological list of
Beethoven's works by writing down in three separate columns
the compositions for piano solo, for orchestra, and for chamber music will ascertain — not without a certain surprise —
how important pieces for piano are almost entirely lacking
from 1805 onward, and quite unrepresented from 1809, until
1816, save two sonatas. Contrariwise, the orchestral production, timid and rare during the first period, suddenly
starts up luxuriantly in this same year 1805, and absorbs the
Master's thoughts to the wellnigh total neglect of his chamber music, wherein he excels. Three trios and five quartets,
that is all that one discovers from 1804 to 1812; whereas the
same eight years have produced no fewer than twenty-four
considerable works for orchestra. Suddenly, one might
almost say, Beethoven exteriorizes his music and seeks to
impress the hearer's emotionality through the effect of
sonority itself. One might, therefore, be tempted to date his
change of style from this year 1804, in which the transformation is manifested by such a rapid and complete evolution
into the instrumental symphony. At all events, an attentive
observer will readily perceive that we must go back to the
year 1801 for the beginnings of this break with the processes previously employed, the shaking off of all indolence
of imitation. It is, in fact, more especially in the sonatas
composed from 1801 to 1804 that one may observe these
hesitations, this uncertainty now so profoundly sorrowful,

BEETHOVEN IN 1804
Painted by Mähler
(Property of Mrs. Heimler, grand-niece of Beethoven)

now tempestuously impassioned, which denote a re-orientation, one might almost say combat, in the creative soul, whereof the sonatas Op. 57 and 53, and the Third Symphony, mark the close.

Before trying to determine the causes of this brusque change, we may be permitted to enumerate its effects upon the style of composition; the captivating interest attaching to this epoch, hitherto quite insufficiently studied, may (we trust) justify in our readers' eyes whatever slight aridity may inhere in a technical digression.

We know that the Sonata, a form of composition growing out of the old Suite of dances, is built up by combining three or four pieces of contrasted type. The first piece (movement) develops a conflict between two themes or musical ideas, which, appearing successively at opposite poles of the adopted tonality, pursue, evade, display each other, and finish by joining together in a common musical *locus* — the tonality just mentioned. This is the "sonata-form" established by Corelli and C. Ph. E. Bach. It still serves at the present time in all serious musical constructive work.

The second piece, ordinarily the slow movement, presents the song-form type divided into three or five sections and based on a theme essentially different from those employed in the sonata-form of the first movement. The third, moderate in tempo, is a survival of the minuet in the old Suite. The fourth, lively and dashing, had adopted, during the greater part of the eighteenth century, the type of the French Rondeau with its refrains and periodical couplets.

The combination of these four types (with some variants, notably in the case of Haydn) constituted at that time the conventional form of the Sonata. After this model were patterned the incipient Symphony (orchestral sonata) and the chamber-music forms.

During the course of his first period Beethoven scrupulously conformed to custom, limiting himself to an occasional imitation of Haydn, who preferred to construct his sonatas in three movements.

But from 1801 onward Beethoven seems to abandon all these rules, and to enter on a new path. Twice he experiments in writing sonatas in which not even a trace remains of the sonata-form: Op. 26, and Op. 27, No. 1. Somewhat later, realizing the necessity for a solid framework in composition, he will again throw himself almost frenziedly upon the sonata-form, as though he would proclaim it to the exclusion of all others (Sonata, Op. 51; Quartets VII, VIII and IX; the four movements of the seventh quartet are written in this form). As early as 1802 he proscribes the Rondo, which will appear but seldom in his works of the second period; he will soon abolish it totally in his sonatas and quartets, not yet venturing to touch the structure of the Symphony; but he sets in the stead of both the moribund Minuet and the roguish Rondo the *Scherzo*, a type all his own, which he in time will exalt into an epopee.

Heretofore he has followed steadily and unquestioningly in the footsteps of his predecessors; and, behold! he all at once breaks the bonds of convention and is swept hither and thither across the traveled way as if by a whirlwind, without the power, at least for a time, of holding a constant course. Hitherto, the signification of his themes has been purely musical, and when he calls himself "pathetic," his care for the arrangement occupies him more than the expression; whereas, at the epoch in which we are now interested, themes and disposition seem to proceed out of unheard-of aberrations which would lead into disorder were he not armed from childhood with a sane and solid education.

Heretofore, he has written merely music; now, it is life whereof he writes.

What can have happened to bring about such a change in Beethoven? Simply this: In the course of his thirty-first year the passions which had (so to speak) only caressed his earlier youth, fell upon him and dragged him into their mad whirl.

He has felt, he has loved, he has suffered. And, perhaps without fully realizing it, he has found himself in a manner forced to fix in his music his impressions, his emotions, his sufferings. His music permits our gaze to penetrate, as through a transparent surface, into the depths of his soul. In his frenzy he unveils the three loves which fill that soul to overflowing in this second period of his career — the love of woman, of nature, of country. And these three loves were what they had to be in so mighty a genius — of a vehemence mounting into passion, delirium. And then add to these heart-surges the uneasiness caused by the first symptoms of the infirmity which was soon — it may be, for the greatest good of Art — to cut him off from all communication with his kind; thus we may arrive at a comprehension of the expansion, the exuberance, of his Second Period.

Only the Largo in Sonata Op. 10, No. 3, written during the first months of 1798, when his deafness, till then benignant, began to grow worse, — this Largo, far more pathetic than the entire Pathetic Sonata, and altogether in the First Manner, gives us a foretaste of what the Second is to be.

But, commencing with 1801, one might reconstruct Beethoven's life almost step by step out of his works.

We shall not undertake any such autobiographical chronology, contenting ourselves with pointing out the principal manifestations of the three grand passions.

THE LOVE OF WOMAN

Beethoven, a being eminently chaste and of deep Christian conviction, could not conceive sensual love otherwise than according to the commandments of God — solely in marriage. He expressed sincerest aversion for such of his colleagues as boasted (after the manner of the time) of some adulterous relation. He severely censured Mozart for having devoted his talents to a description of Don Juan's illicit amours; and, as we have seen, one of the causes which decided him to choose the mediocre book of *Fidelio* was the opportunity it offered of celebrating conjugal love. Hence, small wonder that his life furnishes no romantic liaison, no disorderly adventure, no criminal passion. No; in this line there were no great *external* events whatsoever in his career. He had something better; the torments of a soul ravaged by feminine charm, the violent passion suffered for women whom he could not wed, the deceitful incapacity of even distinctly hearing the voice of the beloved — all this became music and was translated into masterworks.

It was in April, 1800, in the spring of his thirtieth year, that, "for the first time," love, passionate, compelling love, ravished and tortured the soul of Beethoven. In the preceding chapter we told of the coquetries of little Countess Guicciardi, the repulsed offer of marriage (summer of 1802),

[46]

and the crisis of despair which found expression in the Testament of Heiligenstadt. But another testament — one in music — had sealed the tomb of this first love: the Sonata Op. 27, in C♯ minor.

This sonata is the first indication of the agitation excited in Beethoven's spirit by incipient passion; for the first time he expresses his life by his art. It also marks the outset of that troublous period in the order of composition which we mentioned above. Within this poor great man everything is in a ferment, disorganized. He, the believer, seems for an instant to have entertained the notion of suicide. He, the artist nurtured on tradition, seems to revolt against that fecund form to which, nevertheless, he will return speedily and wellnigh exclusively.

Now it is the Sonata in D minor Op. 31, No. 2, very close to the testament of Heiligenstadt both in date and intention; again it is the Sonata in F minor, Op. 57, composed in 1804 after the marriage of Giulietta Guicciardi — a terrible outcry of distress and despair, assuaged by gazing upward "beyond the stars," and ending in a triumphant fanfare. We may be permitted to dwell for a moment on this sonata (entitled, by the grace of a publisher, the "appassionata"). No pianist should venture on its interpretation unless he himself has suffered. To us this appears to be one of Beethoven's most characteristic works from an autobiographical point of view. In this first movement, these two themes that seem made one for the other, proceeding as they do in the same rhythm and the same harmonic character, and which finish, after a constant depression, by distorting and destroying each other — do they not typify the doleful romance of the year 1802, and far more clearly than the so-called "Moonlight Sonata"? After a tranquil, almost religious, petition, passion again seizes him — fiery, yet this time blended with the ardor of soaring aspiration; — and in the final victory, proclaimed by an inadequate piano which ought to be horns, trumpets and cymbals all in one, do we not hear him cry, "It is I! At last, I once more am Beethoven!"

To Schindler, who as a good Philistine asked him what the two sonatas Op. 31 and 57 meant, Beethoven replied: "Read *The Tempest*, by Shakespeare." But in vain shall we seek for Caliban, not to say Prospero, in these flights of passion; the blast of this tempest rages neither on the island nor on the ocean, it breaks loose in a heart, a suffering heart that groans, loves and triumphs.

Finally, how many appeals to a loving and compassionate being, how many agonized complaints, how much of sorrowful resignation, may one find in the compositions written between 1806 and 1815! The Adagio of the seventh quartet, the eighth almost in its entirety, the mysterious Largo of the second trio to Countess Erdödy (Op. 70), "Clärchen" in *Egmont*, the first movement of the eleventh quartet, and, finally, the "Elegischer Gesang" (Op. 118) written in memory of the young Countess Pasqualati, the wife of the friend who during a number of years bestowed on the composer the reposeful shelter of his house.

A matter worthy our notice, which is an outcome of an examination of the works of the Second Period, is that all among these compositions which tell of or reveal amorous anguish can apparently be traced, chronologically speaking, only to his passion for Giulietta Guicciardi. Neither Theresa

GIULIETTA GUICCIARDI
1801

(Miniature, once the property of Beethoven)

Malfatti, nor Amalie Sebald, nor Bettina Brentano, nor the other women whom Beethoven might have noticed, have left any impression on his musical production. But after all, while reading the sonata in $C\sharp$ minor, or the Appassionata, we do not think of the brunette countess with blue eyes, or of woman in any guise; how can one see any other person than the artist-creator himself, who complains, who revolts, or turns away to seek consolation in the woods or smiling meadows?

Still, among the women who were Beethoven's friends, there was one whose name should be mentioned here, were it only to contradict the newly-created legend concerning her. We refer to Countess Therese von Brunswick and her mysterious betrothal to Beethoven.

Throughout the discussions inspired by this romance there is one factor, the most important of all, of which no musico-graph has taken notice — Music. What artist, what man gifted with the simplest artistic perception, would for a moment admit that the sole work dedicated to Countess von Brunswick, the insipid sonata in $F\sharp$ major, Op. 78, could be addressed to the same person as the passionate love-letters which all the world has read? A collection of uninteresting piano-passages, this sonata, which appears to have been written with an eye to some virtuose specialist, is doubtless the most insignificant product of the entire Second Period. This view finds confirmation in the discovery made by M. de Gerando of a long love-correspondence between his great-aunt Therese von Brunswick and a certain Ludwig Migazzi, a distinguished Orientalist. By Therese's own admission, "this love consumed her heart." The publication of the countess's Memoirs, in which Beethoven's name is so rarely mentioned, furnishes further corroboration of this opinion.*

But even were there brought to the support of the betrothal-legend more serious documents than the fantastic narrative written (it is said) by a lady's maid, we should answer No, a hundred times no! These two piano-pieces in expressionless imitation, without musical interest, could never have been the homage of the Titan Beethoven to his "immortal beloved." All that is Music would rise up in testimony to this!

At this juncture one will do well to observe the important and highly significant rôle played by the Dedication in the history of Beethoven's art. Never did the Master of Bonn lightly inscribe a name at the head of a work. This documentary source is indeed most instructive.

Apart from a few necessary and traditional complimentary dedications to crowned heads, all the *important* works that issued from Beethoven's pen — with no exception — are dedicated to those who entered into his life as devoted friends, or affectionate patrons, or intelligent interpreters. To Prince Lichnowsky, who welcomed him at the outset of his career, the three trios, Op. 1; to his master Haydn, the first three piano-sonatas; to his protector in Bonn, the archbishop Max Franz, the first symphony (but, the elector having died before the symphony was published, it was Baron Swieten, one of his earliest Viennese friends, who received the final dedication). Furthermore, in brief, to him who had encouraged his budding talent, Count Waldstein, and

* A recently issued worklet by M. de Hevesy exposes the fragility of the hypotheses so ingeniously constructed by German musicologists with regard to the suppositious loves of Beethoven and Therese.

his dear friend Franz von Brunswick, the sonatas Op. 53 and 57; to his benefactors Lobkowitz and Rasoumowsky, the symphony in *C* minor and the Pastoral Symphony; to Countess Erdödy — we have told what she was for him — the three trios, Op. 70, and the two sonatas for violoncello, Op. 102; to his friend Count Moritz Lichnowsky, that Opus 90 mentioned shortly before; to Baron von Stutterheim (who had accepted Carl, the great man's scapegrace of a nephew, as a cadet in the regiment *Erzherzog Ludwig*, of which he was the colonel), the admirable fourteenth quartet; and to his unique pupil, "dear Archduke" Rudolph of Austria, a long list of masterworks, among them the concerto in *E♭*, the sonata called "Les Adieux," the violin-sonata, Op. 96, the trio, Op. 97, the sonatas Op. 106 and 111, and the Missa solemnis.

Evidently, Beethoven took care (save some royal and imperial exceptions) not to attach the name of any person indifferent to his art to any of his great works. Ferdinand Ries had constituted himself a bodyguard to the great man and remained close to him for many years; but, although an impeccable virtuoso with regard to the *digital* execution of the greatest difficulties, he was of Semitic origin, and could not penetrate into the arcanum of the master's essentially Aryan music. Hence, Beethoven was unwilling to dedicate anything to Ries (or to Moscheles, for the same reason); but to Frau Ertmann, a pianist who admirably interpreted his emotions, he dedicated the Sonata Op. 101; and to Marie Bigot, another interpreter after his own heart, he offered the manuscript of the Appassionata as a gift. We do not find the name of Schindler — the famulus whose devotion was like that of a faithful dog — at the head of a single piece, though he may have deserved better things than the epithets Beethoven showered upon him when aggravated by his want of tact, musical and otherwise; yet the latter, even on his deathbed, could readily recognize goodness of heart in another Vienna burgher, the merchant-draper Wolfmeier, by the dedication of the sixteenth quartet. Bettina herself, the illustrious, flighty Bettina, received the dedication of only an unimportant *Lied*; whereas the name of Brentano figures at the head of Sonata Op. 109, and the superb variations on a theme by Diabelli, one of the great works of the Third Period.

Aside from Sonata Op. 7, inscribed first of all to Woelffl, and afterwards to an ephemeral love, Babette von Keglevics, one can find but a single love-offering amongst all Beethoven's works — the sonata to Giulietta Guicciardi. We have proved that Op. 78, dedicated to Therese von Brunswick, can not be thus characterized. As to the Fourth Symphony, which superficial critics have sought to consider as inspired by the noble countess, its dedication is to Count von Oppersdorf, who ordered it of Beethoven. Now, it was in gratitude to that nobleman for the welcome extended to the symphony in *D* and to himself, in his château at Glogau, that Beethoven inscribed to Oppersdorf the symphony in *B*♭, which he never would have done had the work been an expression of personal sentiments; in this latter case he would have dedicated it to some intimate friend, or would have entirely suppressed the dedication, as he did for Op. 110.

As mentioned above, from 1805 onward Beethoven wrote but little for the piano, fascinated as he was by the attractive corruscations of the orchestra. Two sonatas must, nevertheless, be excepted. They were dictated by friendship, and, although the traditional form is preserved in each of their movements, these compositions grow, in accord with their titles, into veritable poems for the piano.

The Sonata of *l'Adieu* (not at all *"les Adieux,"* as people persist in calling it), with its *Lebewohl* penetrating through all until the parting; the sorrowful plaint of *l'Absence* and the tender caresses of *le Retour*, are most aptly designed to evoke a picture of two lovers, separated, to be reunited in pure and fond embrace. However, the work had a wholly different origin. Archduke Rudolph, while fleeing in 1809 before the French invasion, himself suggested to his Master the sketch for this composition, and from this Beethoven constructed a masterwork which surpasses by far the proposed theme, the "separation of two friends," since it became not merely "an occasional piece such as any man of talent might write" (as the clairvoyant critic of the *Allgemeine musikalische Zeitung* expressed it in 1812), but the musical type of every farewell, of every absence, of every return. — O imaginative might of genius, which, to create the New, needed not to repudiate the old forms!

The history of Sonata Op. 90 is no less curious. It was Beethoven's intention (as he himself indicated) to depict musically the romance of his friend Moritz Lichnowsky. This friend, infatuated with an actress, and torn betwixt love and prejudices, hesitated for a long time, suffering greatly from his indecision, until love won the day and a happy marriage resulted. The two pieces constituting the sonata follow this situation, so to speak, step by step. The impetuosity of the first movement, in which the character of Count Moritz, marked alike by pride and weakness, is so clearly drawn from the outset ("combat between head and heart"), forms an admirable antithesis to the very tender charm of the finale ("converse with the loved one"). Here Beethoven, resuming — after so long abandonment — the ancient form of the Rondo, attempts to depict, by means of the frequent recurrence of the constant refrain, the fond and enduring monotony of that conjugal happiness which was the dream, never to be realized, of his life.

The Love of Nature

For Beethoven, Nature was not merely a consoler in his sorrows and his disenchantments, but a friend with whom he delighted to hold intimate converse — the sole intercourse to which his deafness raised no obstacle.

How did the author of the Pastoral Symphony see and conceive Nature? Not, assuredly, in the dry theoretical fashion of Rousseau, whose writings on the natural education were none the less one of the sensations of the time; what point of contact could subsist between the Genevan Calvinist and the effusions of a Beethoven, Catholic by birth and culture? Neither was it at all after the manner in which the Romanticists had already begun to treat the fields, forests and plains. Beethoven never looked upon Nature as "immense, impenetrable and proud," in the way of Berlioz (speaking through the mouth of his Faust). A little nook in a valley, a meadow, a tree, sufficed for Beethoven; so thoroughly could he penetrate natural beauties that, for more than twelve years, all his music was as if impregnated with them; as for pride, there could be no question of that beside this indulgent friend, this discreet confidante of his woes and his joys. Yes, indeed, Beethoven loves Nature

[54]

ardently, and can show her to us through the prism of an artist-heart, a heart full of tenderness and kindness, aiming at a single end — to elevate himself and, through his love for Creation, penetrate to the Creator: "In the fields I seem to hear every tree repeating 'Holy! Holy! Holy!'"

Shortly after the terrible crisis caused by his love for Giulietta Guicciardi, there might have been seen on Beethoven's table a book which, during twelve years, was his favorite volume, the "Lehr- und Erbauungs-Buch" of Sturm. The underscored passages in this work, so well thumbed that he was obliged to procure a second copy, permit of no doubt with respect to the assertion just put forward. Still better, he himself copied, that it might be ever-present to sight and thought, the following passage from the book in question: "One might rightly denominate Nature the school of the heart; she clearly shows us our duties towards God and our neighbor. Hence, I wish to become a disciple of this school and to offer Him my heart. Desirous of instruction, I would seek after that wisdom which no disillusionment can confute; I would gain a knowledge of God, and through this knowledge I shall obtain a foretaste of celestial felicity."

Now, precisely what may have been this Nature beloved of Beethoven, the moving cause of so many masterworks, this countryside which evoked such lofty inspirations? Why, nothing more nor less than the nature of his immediate neighborhood, the open country through which he could ramble familiarly on his daily walks. While Beethoven was an indefatigable pedestrian, to the point of sometimes harshly rejecting offers to accompany him, he was never what is nowadays termed an excursionist. The tourist "fad," this mania of modern Germany, which has reached the pitch (with the concurrent instinct for militarization) of investing itself in a uniform (a grayish green sack-coat with staghorn buttons, and an ugly little hat with tufted tassel), this tourist fad, we repeat, did not exist at the beginning of the nineteenth century. When one undertook a long journey, it was for business, not recreation; but short excursions afoot were in great vogue.

At that period — and still at the present time — the small hamlets in the vicinity of the larger German towns were dotted with cheery *Wirthschaften* (taverns), not as yet ticketted with the pompous barbarism *Restauration*. These inviting publics opened their friendly doors in fine weather to the crowd of burghers from the towns, who, famishing for a breath of fresh country air, had the satisfaction of encountering on the wooden tables the habitual sausage escorted by the traditional *Schoppen* of beer. Each hospitable cabaret found its completion in a dance-hall wherein a very limited orchestra regulated the prancing of ruddy-cheeked *Burschen* and sentimental *Mägdlein*, while a discreet garden offered, between dances, its perfumed walks for amorous effusions. Out beyond the suburban village — the more decent and less noisy equivalent of our Asnières or our Robinson — stretched the real country; cultivated fields, narrow valleys, with streams issuing tranquilly from nearby heights, and almost everywhere, quite near at hand, a real forest of century-old trees whose shadows invited revery. Here one left the domain of the holiday-making citizen to enter that of the peasant, who similarly celebrated his rest-days in drinking, dancing and singing. But songs and dances took on a far ruder and more characteristic aspect

[56]

DÖBLING, AT THE FOOT OF THE KAHLENBERG
(Aquarelle, cover of box)

beneath this open sky than in the tepid atmosphere of the suburban tavern.

Whether in the immediate environs of Vienna — at Döbling, at Heiligenstadt, at Penzing, Mödling, Hetzendorf — or in the vicinity of the towns whose sulphurous or alkaline waters invited him when in ill health, and only excepting the parks *à la française* of certain princely mansions, such was the landscape which everywhere met Beethoven's eye during his rambles, now north or west of Vienna, now in the plain watered by the Wien, or skirting the rocks of Baden, or beneath the great fir-trees of Teplitz.

But among all these rural nooks, the one most fertile in inspiration for Beethoven is, incontestably, that extending northward from the Austrian capital to the slopes of the Kahlenberg and Leopoldsberg. When he hired for the summer a cottage in Döbling or Grinzing or Heiligenstadt (as yet not promoted to the grade of official suburbs), the Master had to walk but a short distance to find himself in the open country. Turning to the right, just after passing the last houses in Heiligenstadt, he descended into the Wild-grube (a narrow, green valley) by a footpath which is still called the *Beethovengang* (Beethoven Path), and stayed his steps beside the brook of the Sixth Symphony, the placid and shady Schreiberbach. Here he found himself about midway between the burgher waltzes and the peasant songs, and in several of his works he notes this bizarre antithesis. Would he push on yet further? He crossed the brook at a bound or, in the season of freshets, on a shaky plank, and ascended the sloping hillside through an unbroken forest. After pausing, perhaps, halfway up for refreshment at the sign of the Iron Hand, he sought out the villagers on their native heath, in the hamlet of Kahlenberg, and sometimes strolled even a league further, to the rustic town of Weidling. So it must have been within the narrow limits of some eight or ten miles either to the north of Vienna, or at Baden or Hetzendorf, that were conceived and written (or, at least, sketched) not a single "Pastoral Symphony" but ten pastoral symphonies, that is to say, ten great works, at the fewest, telling of Beethoven's impressions face to face with Nature.

First of all, according to date, the charming sonata for piano Op. 28 (entitled "pastoral" in some editions). This work (antedating, despite the number, his Op. 27) seems like the avowal to fields and forests of a moment of calm happiness, at the dawn of his love for "la Damigella Contessa Giulietta di Guicciardi." Then come the sonatas Op. 30, No. 3 (for violin, to Emperor Alexander) and Op. 31, No. 3 (for piano, 1802-1803); the admirable sonata in C major, Op. 53, which the Germans call the Waldstein-Sonate, and the French "l'Aurore," contemporary with and, so to speak, consolatory for the tortures of Op. 57; then three movements out of four in the seventh quartet (1806), and the Sixth, Seventh and Eighth Symphonies; finally, the superb tenth sonata for violin, Op. 96, in its entirety (1812); without taking account of the rustic dances, the finales of the trios Op. 70, No. 2, and Op. 97, or the pastoral entr'acte in *Egmont*.

While an analysis of each of these genial productions will hardly be expected here, it will be to the reader's advantage to observe that it was never a material impression, the realistic reproduction of sounds tuneful or noisy of the countryside, which Beethoven sought to express in his music, but solely the spirit of the country as it penetrated the heart of the artist and was transmuted into sonorous forms by his intelligence.

Let us rapidly trace the genesis of the Sixth Symphony. — How does Beethoven succeed in suggesting to us the calm of the fields, the soul's tranquillity in contact with Nature? By means of harmonic agglomerations ingeniously arranged, which may satisfy curiosity, but do not touch the heart? Oh, far from it! He will seek, and seeking will find, a simple melody; and the compass of the melodic design, limited to excess (for it embraces only the interval of a sixth, from *F* to *D*)*, will suffice to induce within us a feeling of calm both by its comparative immobility and by the duration of this immobility. In fact, the exposition of this melody founded on the interval of a sixth fills fifty-two measures of uninterrupted repetitions in different timbres, but musically identical. Wagner will utilize later an analogous procedure to portray the monotonous majesty of the river, in the introduction to *Das Rheingold*. The second idea in this first movement of the Pastoral Symphony is duplex. We might liken it to the appearance, in the heretofore inanimate landscape, of two human beings, a man and a woman, strength and tenderness. This second idea forms the thematic base of the whole work. In the Scherzo, the effect of a sudden cessation of motion produced by the tune on the strolling musician's bagpipe (the solo for oboe, then for horn), and

* In his "Essais de technique et d'esthétique musicales" (1902, pp. 380–383) M. Élie Poirée has already remarked on the pastoral character of this interval in the tonality of *F* major, which he explains, through a very plausible phenomenon of "color-audition," as corresponding to the color green.

overcoming the noisy merriment of the peasants, is due to the cause stated above; though in the present case the melody, save for one note, proceeds within the range of a fifth.

The storm which interrupts the villagers' assembly makes no pretence of frightening us. Far from letting loose all the known instruments of percussion, and inventing new ones at need, Beethoven contents himself with the insufficient kettledrums to reproduce the rolling of the thunder; but, after all, he does better. Have you noticed, that in four pieces out of the five of which the symphony is composed, there is not a passage, not a fragment of development, established in a minor tonality? That is why this key of *F* minor, held in reserve for the gloom overspreading the landscape until then flooded with sunshine and gayety, produces, in every soul poetically endowed, the inevitable sense of oppression, of distressful uneasiness, which accompanies the approach of a thunderstorm. Then, too, what a burst of light, how freely one breathes when the blue sky reappears with the theme that preceded the storm, in the same *ambitus* of a sixth whose tranquil significance was revealed to us in the commencement of the symphony! Now a shepherd's song is heard, ushering in an explosion of joy; and these two themes are nothing more nor less than the two elements, masculine and feminine, developed in the first movement.

We have intentionally withheld, for the close of this succinct analysis, the Andante, the most admirable expression of genuine nature in existence; there are only a few passages in Wagner's *Siegfried* and *Parsifal* that may be compared with it. — Conductors generally err by taking this Andante too slowly, thereby impairing its alert poetic spirit; and yet the composer wrote the careful direction "Molto moto, quasi allegretto." It is a veritable model of construction in sonata-form. While the flow of the stream provides a plastic foundation for the entire movement, lovely melodies expressively rise up out of it, and the feminine theme of the initial Allegro reëmerges alone, as though uneasy at its companion's absence. Each section in the movement is completed by the entrance of a theme of a few notes, pure as a prayer. It is the artist who speaks, who prays, who loves, and who takes delight in crowning the divisions of his work with a sort of Alleluia. This expressive theme terminates the expositions, twines about the steps of the development, in the midst of which the obscure tonalities cause a shadow to pass over the land; then, following the somewhat puerile episodes of the bird-songs, it is again thrice repeated, to conclude the whole with a touching affirmation.

Space forbids our speaking of the sonata Op. 53 — eminently *pastoral* in the sense which Beethoven attached to the word. Curiously enough, the theme of the finale of this sonata, which seems so perfectly simple, is one of those whose definitive shaping required the greatest efforts; Beethoven's sketch-books present its final form only after six sketches very different in rhythm and even in melody.

The symphony in *A*, which the musicologists (following Wagner) have baptized "the apotheosis of the dance," is a pastoral symphony pure and simple. In the rhythm of the first movement there is certainly nothing dance-like; it seems rather as if inspired by the song of a bird. The trio in the Scherzo reproduces, it is said, the melody of a pilgrims' chant heard at Teplitz in 1812; and the finale is a village festival aptly characterized.

The Eighth Symphony also evidently retraces impressions received from Nature. The trio of the pompous Minuet, where clarinet, violoncello and horn carry on an almost grotesque passage at arms, does it not represent a peasants' band? And the Hungarian theme — the hymn of Hunyadi — which appears periodically in the finale, does it not imitate the arrival of itinerant musicians, Gypsies, in the midst of a festival?

But the work which, together with the Sixth Symphony, most vividly awakens in our soul a sensation as of the smiling Austrian countryside, is the sonata for piano and violin in G major, Op. 96. In the first movement one already feels the caresses of a soft breeze; and although troops twice march by in the distance, one speedily forgets the panoply of war in the fair dream-landscape evoked by the music. The Adagio, in song-form, is a real masterpiece of penetrating melody, a reverie on a wooded slope which would be a fitting pendant to that "on the bank of a brook." It does not reach completion; a peasant festival, serving as a Scherzo, suddenly breaks in upon the reverie. And there is nothing more curious than this Scherzo. In it Beethoven, perhaps for the first time, becomes descriptive. Lying in a meadow, or maybe perched in a tree, the poet at first notes a dance of countryfolk in rough, almost barbarous rhythms — the Scherzo; then from another quarter there come to his ear, now louder, now fainter, as if borne on gusts of wind, the echoes of a burgher dance — a *valse noble*, as Schumann would have said — which soon give way in turn, as befits a good classic trio, to the Scherzo *redivivus*. And this little descriptive tableau for two opposites is not unique among Beethoven's works; the same form, though less completely expressed, will be met with in the finale to Op. 53, in the trios Op. 70 and 97, and, lastly, in the Minuet of the Eighth Symphony, mentioned before. This admirable sonata for violin, the last written by Beethoven for that instrument, and too often played in a style subversive of its true sense, is like a résumé of the trio in $B\flat$, likewise dedicated to the Archduke. We do not hesitate to place this famous trio also among those of Beethoven's works which were inspired by his ardent love of Nature — almost equal in its productivity of masterworks, during this second period of his creative life, to his love of Woman.

His Love of Country

Beethoven dearly loved his "unique German Fatherland"; his letters, and his touching returns in imagination to the borders of Father Rhine, furnish the proof. But there can be no doubt that he equally cherished the land of his adoption, Austria; — and how could it well be otherwise when he shared, morally and materially, in her woes, her anguish, her distresses, ending in final triumph?

But what was his share, as an artist, in this sentiment? In what aspect, musically speaking, did the author of the Heroic Symphony view his country? In a word, what mode of procedure did it please him to adopt for the expression of his patriotism in music? His procedure was borrowed, incontestably, from the "military mode," or (if you prefer) the adaptation of a warlike rhythm to the melody. This familiar rhythm — a dotted eighth-note followed by a sixteenth — was then, and still is, the proper thing in all military affairs where music can play a part; triumphal or funeral marches, infantry charges, assaults, even retreats; and this rhythmic form retained its specialized application until Meyerbeer diverted it therefrom to employ it indiscriminatingly in his operas. Why wonder at such military expression of patriotism in Beethoven, whose entire life, excepting the last ten years, was passed in the very midst of war, amid bombardments, invasions, the movements of armies? Does it not seem natural that his conception of country should have been inseparable from the martial display by which he was surrounded, and that the somewhat grandiloquent heroism after the manner of Plutarch, his favorite author, should be materialized for Beethoven in the shape of gigantic plumes and Hungarian kurtkas, and find musical expression in the rhythms of the drum-beat and gallop?

We encounter it in this shape in the dead-march of Op. 26; in the violin-sonata dedicated to Emperor Alexander, Op. 30, No. 2, where the second theme assumes the guise of an attack by the Preobajenski grenadiers; in the Third Symphony; in the violin-concerto (1806); in the warlike Andante and so absolutely heroic finale of the Fifth Symphony (1808); in the overture and entr'actes to *Egmont* (1809), and, very naturally, in the "Victory of Wellington" and the dozen marches or pieces for military band which he wrote from 1809 to 1816. One can still find echoes or reminiscences of it in Op. 101 (1816), and as late as the fifteenth quartet and the Ninth Symphony.

To a certain extent this martial spirit again reveals itself in the superb overture to *Coriolanus* (1807), although the military rhythm does not appear; but here this spirit en-

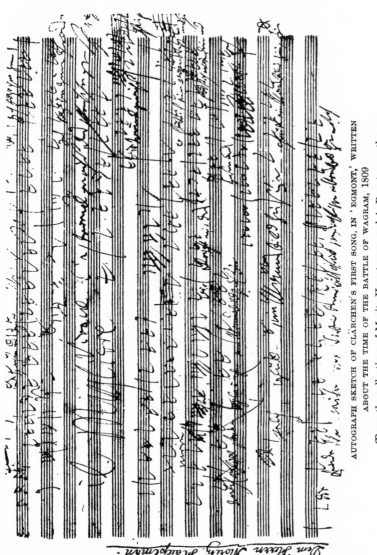

AUTOGRAPH SKETCH OF CLÄRCHEN'S FIRST SONG, IN 'EGMONT,' WRITTEN
ABOUT THE TIME OF THE BATTLE OF WAGRAM, 1809

(From the collections of Moritz Hauptmann and A. Bovet, now the
property of M. Vincent d'Indy)

gages in conflict with an admirable theme of conjugal love, and ends, like the hero of the drama, by succumbing to the buffets of fate.

Here we must interpose an observation apropos of the Heroic Symphony. We agree perfectly with the opinion expressed by M. Chantavoine in his essay on Beethoven; it appears to us beyond doubt that the name of Bonaparte, inscribed by the musician on the title-page of the symphony, was so placed in the sense of a dedication. In fact, the composition of the Third Symphony coincides with that quite restricted period of Beethoven's career in which he addressed the dedications of important works to heads of the State. The first two sonatas for violoncello were dedicated, as early as 1796, to the king of Prussia, Frederick William II; in 1799, Beethoven inscribed the great septet (Op. 20) to the empress Maria Theresa; in 1802, three violin-sonatas to the emperor of Russia. So it is not astonishing that in 1804 he desired to offer one of his great compositions to the head of the French State; and no one would ever dream of discussing the origin of the Third Symphony, had not political toadyism seized upon it in the obstinate endeavor to make Beethoven appear in some sort as an apostle of the Revolution.

While his contemporaries seem not even to have suspected that the origin of the *Eroica* might be sought elsewhere than in the tableaux of warfare with which the Vienna newspapers were then filled — witness Czerny or Dr. Bertolini, his intimate friends, who fancied it to depict a naval battle, Aboukir, or the glorification of Nelson and the English general Abercrombie — poor Schindler, steeped in republican ideology and yielding to the mania for appearing *progressive* (this was in 1840), bethought himself (in his book) of imputing to

Beethoven political intentions. Remarking on the sketches for the work, he compares several passages with Plato's "Republic," which the great musician, he says, was particularly fond of reading; — never suspecting that Beethoven, in 1803, could not be acquainted with this work, the first German translation (by Schleiermacher) having been published at Berlin long after the Heroic Symphony had been produced at Vienna.

Besides, even if Beethoven had been a follower of Plato, and had passed his time, as the conversation-tablets indicate, in grumbling with impunity at Court and Town, in declaring the police meddlesome, justice halting, the administration bound in red tape (and what Frenchman of that day or this could not "give him points" in these matters?), how does all that imply "republican opinions" in the modern sense of the term? Does any one know that he did not seek, in Plato's book, the theory of the ancient Greek modes rather than a model for a democratic constitution? But it was left for writers of our own time to improve on Schindler's hypothesis and to present us with a Beethoven not merely enamoured of Plato's Republic, but eager to glorify the French Revolution in a lump, including the September massacres, the Terror, etc. — Everything we know about what the Master loved, and what he hated, about his hatred as an exiled patriot for the revolutionary invasion, rises up against such an interpretation. Jacobinism could be only repugnant to his honest heart. And this hypothesis, conceived quite without reference to historical considerations, has not even the excuse of supporting itself by dates. For at the time when Beethoven wrote and dedicated his symphony under the leafy shades of Ober-Döbling, that is to say, from 1803 to 1804, it was no longer the spokesman of the Revolution, the redoutable consummater of the principles of '89, who met his sight, but far rather the glorious hero crowned with laurels, the vigorous soldier, vanquisher of anarchy, who with a gesture, and by a formal violation of the republican constitution, had just "assassinated national representation";* he to whom he inscribed the Heroic Symphony was the Man of Brumaire.

The dead-march, the sole movement of the Third Symphony in which one finds the "military rhythm" spoken of above, appears to have been conceived, not at all on the occasion of "the death of a hero," like the one in Op. 26, but with intent to celebrate all the heroes who, falling for their country, held fast even in death to the hope of a supra-terrestrial life. In 1821, Beethoven observed jestingly that he had spoken Napoleon's funeral oration seventeen years before the decease of the captive of St. Helena. This same funeral oration might well have been applied to his own case, for at the close of their lives these two great men suffered a similar fate — both isolated; the man of war on an isle of the ocean, the musician in an art inaccessible to the masses; both separated from the rest of the world, the artist of genius by his terrible infirmity, like the fallen conqueror by the inexorable sea and the no less inexorable Britain.

Among the series of some forty *Lieder* which appeared during this period of Beethoven's life, there is little worthy of special attention. We shall mention only the Sacred Songs, Op. 48, on words by Gellert; then the "Wachtel-schlag" (Quail's Cry), a sort of invocation to God on the rhythm of this bird's call; in this highly developed *Lied*

* Memoirs of Barras.

not one of the six verses is set like a preceding one, and certain modulations go even further than the second manner; the rhythmic refrain, always the same: "Fear God, love God, praise God, thank God, pray to God, trust in God," is like a trial-sketch for the termination of the Andante in the Pastoral Symphony — the birds' prayer completed by a human prayer. "Das Glück der Freundschaft" (The Happiness of Friendship), Op. 88, already evokes that hymn of love which forms the subject of the Ninth Symphony; and in the little duo "Merkenstein," Op. 100, written in 1814, we encounter the familiar landscape of the environs of Baden. Apropos of the *Lieder* it should be observed that their production, very sparse in the period from 1801 to 1808, does not begin to grow abundant until 1809, at the time when Beethoven, abandoning the piano-sonata, is about to devote himself wholly to the enchantments of the orchestra. In the songs, the patriotic note is very pronounced, from the "Warsong of the Austrians," composed in 1797, down to the anti-French pamphlet "All is over," with the intermediate "Warrior's Farewell," "Germania," and the Cantata for the Vienna Congress.

It would be taken amiss, did we fail to speak here of *Leonore, or, Conjugal Love*, Beethoven's sole opera. The first representation of the work took place in 1805; it was revived in 1806; and produced under its original title, *Fidelio*, when newly arranged in two acts for the revival of 1814.

At the risk of provoking Teutonic wrath — for Germany has made a kind of fetish of *Fidelio* — we make bold to say that this opera is very far, very far indeed, from having a value in the dramatic class equal to that, in the purely instrumental style, of the sonatas, the symphonies, and the quartets. The fact must be recognized, that *Fidelio* did not advance, by a single step, the development of dramatic music; it is nothing but an opera, one to which Mozart might have signed his name, one that shows no advancement whatever beyond the operas of the same epoch. Twenty years later *Der Freischütz* and *Euryanthe* gave a quite different impulse to German musical drama. With regard to *Fidelio* it looks as if Beethoven, in attempting this new style, had lost his bearings and was only trying, like a good pupil, to apply the rules he had learned of Salieri, without striving to break with the Italian convention, or even seeking to continue the expressive tradition of Gluck. Most of the melodies, taken separately, are good Beethoven stuff, of course; but the way in which they are brought into action has nothing of novelty, scarcely gives the impression of a drama. In the first act, with the exception of the enthusiastic Allegro of Leonore's aria and the scenic play of the Prisoners' Chorus, there is nothing, or hardly anything, that makes a lasting impression. Musically speaking, the second offers more of interest. Florestan's aria, accompanied after the mode of sixteenth-century airs by an oboe *concertante* (like that of Leonore, in the first act, by the three horns), is simply a suite of two agreeable *Lieder*. The duet in the prison-vault, between Leonore and Rocco, constitutes a genuine sonata with its double exposition and its development. The only dramatically expressive number is that in which the young wife, victorious over Pizarro's rancor, throws herself into her husband's arms, thus bringing on a passionate explosion of the sublime love-phrase which until then had been confined to a merely *hopeful* form.

But that which is incomparable in *Fidelio*, which thrills us afresh with the Beethoven touch, is the music for orchestra alone. Its power of evocation brings us face to face with the dramatic action with far greater force and vividness than the vocal scenes. First of all, the admirable introduction to the second act, which, making us assist and participate in the physical and moral sufferings of the unhappy prisoner, arouses in our souls an emotion more intense than even the aria of Florestan can evoke. Should we, in view of this piece, call the reader's attention to a somewhat curious detail? A certain number of orchestral devices, since employed by divers composers for expressing unhappiness, misfortune, hatred, may be found in this introduction distinctly set out in notes. The expressive scroll which musical treatises have decorated with the ugly name of *gruppetto*, and which appears with similar sorrowful intent in the Adagio of the seventh quartet, is the Wagnerian "turn" anticipated — the plaint of Parsifal on learning the death of his mother Herzeleide; a little further on we have those same *pizzicati* in the double-basses which, in *Der Freischütz*, accompany the entries of Samiel, the Prince of Hate, as Pizarro is its servitor. Not even the foreboding diminished fifth of the giants Fafner and Fasolt in *Rheingold* is missing; it is found where the kettledrums mark the feverish pulsations of the prisoner's heart. This introduction will stand as a masterpiece of dramatic art beside the Death of Clärchen in *Egmont*.

And what shall we say of the three overtures in *C*, wherein the drama *in its entirety* opens to our sight? What shall we say, above all, of the overture designated by the number "3," which Beethoven wrote for the revival of 1806? In

these compositions the theme of lament and the theme of
hope, which are like representatives of the two characters,
come together little by little, following the grievous struggle
with Hatred, and unite, transforming themselves after the
liberating fanfare into an outburst of the most ardent love!

There is still one work we ought to mention, which, without offering great musical interest, possesses nevertheless,
for atavistic reasons, a certain importance. We have already seen how, in a simple *Lied*, the primitive expression
of that *Gegenliebe* (mutual love) was born which occupied
Beethoven's mind during life. The mutual love of man
and woman, the only love portrayed by the melody of 1796,
we shall see transformed into the *Fantasie* for piano, orchestra and chorus, dedicated, in 1808, to the king of Bavaria.
Here the theme of mutual love is presented and developed,
save in a few details, like that in the finale of the Ninth
Symphony, whose ancestor it is beyond cavil. Given out
at first by the piano and the solo instruments of the orchestra,
it obtains its significance, as in the symphony of 1823, only
through the voices of the singers (likewise soloists), which
are then reinforced by the full chorus. The text no longer
describes the attachment of two lovers, but the affinity
which binds great souls together; and — a curious point —
the same modulation, or rather the same *fermata* on the $B\flat$-
major chord which, in the Ninth Symphony, betokens the
abode of the Divine Being, reappears in the same place and
same key towards the end of the Fantasie, to symbolize
"the union of Love and Power" realized in God alone.

In conclusion, what is characteristic in the style of this

Second Period, whose chief manifestations we have just passed in review, may be summed up in a few words: The disturbance caused by the first onset of the passions, finding expression through a period almost disorderly, in a musical sense, from 1801 to 1804. In 1804 the crisis is passed, and equilibrium reëstablished in three masterworks — the sonata Op. 57 (love), Op. 53 (nature), and the Third Symphony (heroism). At last this soul, whether suffering or comforted, feels the need of voicing its woes to the world or of proclaiming to all the kind consolations of Nature; now, *for the first time*, it is the orchestra, that hundred-voiced instrument, which it demands for expressing its exuberant enthusiasm. Thus it happens that Beethoven's entire orchestral production (excepting the two masterworks of 1822 and 1823) belongs to ten short years between 1804 and 1815; seven symphonies, nine overtures, seven concertos or instrumental pieces, four pieces for orchestra with chorus, five pieces for military music, three melodramas, an opera, an oratorio, and a mass. Before these, there was nothing but the First Symphony; after them, only two colossal works in which the orchestra serves rather as a means than as an end. It was necessary to establish this fact for the confusion of those who claim to find in Beethoven absolute unity of style.

From a technical point of view, the observations to be made in support of the total change of manner would be so numerous as to exceed the limits of this volume. We shall content ourselves with noting the considerable modifications which the plan of the Sonata underwent without departing from the traditional route (with Beethoven the sonata tends to become a poem in two cantos), and the changes in the

BEETHOVEN IN 1814

Engraved by Blasius Höfel, after a pencil sketch by Louis Letronne

(The engraving was retouched from the life.)

interior structure of the Symphony, which now calls to its aid instruments until then unemployed (two and three horns, and the trombones), and anon celebrates the appearance of a descriptive piece (the Sixth Symphony), or the addition of a *third theme* (Third Symphony), or the interconnection and reappearance of themes of one piece in another (the Fifth and Sixth Symphonies).

And now the moment has come for us to say, paraphrasing the introductory recitative in the finale of the Ninth: "Friends, let us leave this style; may songs arise, yet more beautiful, striving ever higher towards the Kingdom of God!"

THIRD PERIOD

FROM 1814 TO 1827

V

HIS LIFE

"MY dear, honored friend! You may think, and not without cause, that I have lost all remembrance of you; but it only appears so. My brother's death occasioned me great sorrow, followed by great exertions to rescue my beloved nephew from his unworthy mother. This was successful, but till now I have not been able to do anything better for him than to place him in an Institute, that is, away from me. And what is an Institute compared with the ever-present sympathy and care of a father for his child! For such I now consider myself, and am continually planning how I may take this treasure to myself in order to influence him more directly and advantageously. — But how difficult that is for me! — Besides, for the last six weeks I have been far from well, so that I often have thoughts of death, though without dread, only I should die too soon for my poor Carl. From your last lines to me I see that you too, my dear friend, are in great suffering. That is, indeed, the lot of mankind; in this, too, our strength must be tried, I mean, we must endure without knowing, and feel our nothingness, and again strive after that perfection of which the Almighty may then deem us worthy."

This letter, written to Mme. Erdödy in 1816, sufficiently explains the recent events in the Master's life. Beethoven had unhesitatingly responded to the call of his dying brother. And yet, he has no idea of how to conduct a household or of keeping accounts. What folly, to take charge of a nine-year-old child! — so said his friends. And then the prospect of a continual struggle with the mother, jealous of her rights.

Oh! this Queen of Night, "Jeannette," as she was called by the gay world! How many imprecations will he shower upon her in the course of the long evenings spent in the home of Giannatasio del Rio, the master of the boarding-school! There, at least, they listen to him and pity him. Fanny, the eldest daughter (the "Mother Superior," as he entitles her), keeps house and watches over the health of the little pupils who are so fond of playing at bowls with Herr van Beethoven. Good Fanny! Her conventual title mortifies her somewhat, for she has certain pretensions — and she admires Beethoven so passionately! "Ah! what might one do, at need, for such a man!" she sighs in her diary. "He is so unhappy, and there is no one to console him!"

With regard to Carl's education, Beethoven is in no wise niggardly: "We shall make an artist or a scientist of him, so that he may lead an elevated life, above the vulgar; for only the artist and the free man of learning derive their happiness from within." Hence, Carl will have the best masters; Czerny will teach him the art of piano-playing, and Beethoven will better his teaching: "Above all, keep to the sense of the musical phrase. Although I have taught but little, I have perceived that this is the only method for forming musicians, which, after all, is one objective point of the art." And, as to fingering: "Do not overdo the pearly style; one may like pearls, but occasionally admire other jewels."

Carl will not remain long with Giannatasio; his uncle's purse could not meet the demands of an expensive private school patronized by all the best families of Vienna. There is a growing need of money. For his Carl, Beethoven will protest poverty; he will become a pertinacious mendicant, and will flout as "beggarly" all the princes of earth for their lack of generosity — so he feels it — towards artists. "I am a father," he writes Wegeler, "but without a wife." So let us leave him to struggle with that "allegro di confusione," his household, with the too celebrated governesses Nanni, Pepi and Baberl; here even the obliging Frau Streicher is at her wits' end. Shall we mention the amusing lesson in domestic economy that he makes her give him? — "Do you have to cook things separately?" "When you cook asparagus or any delicate vegetables, of course they ought to be done separately; but when you have only cabbage it is more economical to make one soup for everybody, otherwise you will use double the amount of fat." — "And for breakfast?" "This is fast-day, so we shall have only a thin soup, a bit of fish, and a piece of *Gogelhopf*,* at noon; to-morrow is a holiday, so every one may expect two grilled sausages besides the roast, to say nothing of a glass of wine, you will understand." — "And for the laundry?" — . . .

We shall let Carl go successively to the curate of Mödling, to the Kudlich school, to Blöchlinger, to the Polytechnic

---

* *Gugelhupf* or *Gogelhopf*, a favorite high, round coffee-cake with fluted sides and a hole in the middle; made plain, or with chopped almonds. North German names are *Aschkuchen* and *Napfkuchen*.

Institute, and try literature, philology and business, one
after the other. Nothing turned out as one might have
wished.

Nevertheless, Carl was not a bad boy. Some rather neat
reflections of his are on record; he was a fairly good musician,
with an inclination to poetry and letters: — "You can pro-
pose a riddle in Greek to him," proudly remarked his uncle.
But from his mother he inherited an irresistible penchant
for pleasure. How prevent him from enjoying the cafés,
billiards, balls, and the society of "certain young ladies
nothing less than virtuous" — all matters concerning which
Beethoven understands no jesting. "One night in the
Prater at a ball; slept abroad two nights!" the poor Master
anxiously notes in his memorandum-book. And when Carl
presents fantastic bills for laundry-work, he suspects hidden
debts, he listens to the gossip of the women who let lodgings,
he goes so far as to follow the silly youth to the dance-halls!
Vain surveillance! "I have become less good," Carl writes,
"the more my uncle wanted me to be better." From the
most violent reproaches, Beethoven passes to the expression
of the fondest affection. At Blöchlinger's they overhear
him crying, with all the strength of his poor, infirm lungs,
"You dishonor me! My name is too well known in Vienna
. . . ." and, while speaking, he coughs, spits, and flourishes his
handkerchief, to the great disgust of the object of his lecture.
"Oh! I beg you!" he cries once again, "do not make my poor
heart bleed afresh!" And finally, after the catastrophe of
July the 30th, 1826 (the attempt at suicide, provoked in
great part by his own railing), when Beethoven goes to visit
the "rake" on his bed in the hospital, he murmurs in sup-
plicating accents: "If you have any hidden grief, let me

know it. . . . through your mother." And at this moment, worn out by the solicitude of his all too loving uncle, Carl turns his face to the wall. . . . What a wound for Beethoven's heart! And how many other heartaches were due to the continual "intrigues and treachery" of this same mother! During the course of his lawsuit did she not seize upon the lack of documentary evidence to contest the validity of her brother-in-law's title to the particle "van" which he thought so much of, and so to annul the judgments? What an affront for a man whose anti-democratic sentiments had so often been affirmed! Remember his disdain for the "populasse," the "plebs," that vile multitude stigmatized by Romain Rolland; his "I do not compose for the galleries!" to Baron Braun; and his remark to Hiller: "*Vox populi, vox Dei*, is a proverb that I have never taken seriously."

Henceforward the Master will find the vast capital too narrow for him: "A superior man ought not to be confounded with the ordinary citizens — and I have been!" And he burrows, and frowns on society. Nobody sees him now. He makes a solitary exception in favor of his "gracious lord" Archduke Rudolph, to whom he gives several lessons a week, and who, through this portion of Beethoven's life, seems to cover his master with his protecting shadow.

A great noble of charming mien, enthusiastic and modest, of an almost feminine delicacy. Ever indulgent to the erratic humor of the poor deaf man, listening to his diatribes against the Austrian state, which he accuses of every misdeed from the unsatisfactory work of the servants to the bad draught of the chimneys, the archduke levels before Beethoven, at the imperial palace, all barriers of etiquette. We shall see how he puts himself to the inconvenience of

ARCHDUKE RUDOLPH OF AUSTRIA
(1788–1831)

Cardinal Archbishop of Olmütz

(Gesellschaft der Musikfreunde, Vienna)

looking up, in person, lodgings for Beethoven at Baden, and exerts his influence to find homes for poor musicians recommended by him. At the advent of the Finanz-Patent of 1811 and the bankruptcy reducing the paper florin to one-fifth of its face value, he, with fine generosity, orders that his master shall be paid his full stipend, although not obliged by law to do so, constraining by his example the other parties to the contract and thus, calming Beethoven's impatience, intervening in the proceedings undertaken against Kinsky so as to obtain a happy solution. His testimony is to sustain Beethoven against the calumnies of his sister-in-law when she drags herself to the very feet of the emperor, and against the perfidy of the Jew, Pulai, who boasted that he would ruin the musician in the eyes of the Court by imputing atheistic sentiments to him. "His Imperial Highness knows how scrupulously I have always fulfilled my duties toward God, nature and humanity." So he deserves that Beethoven should write his brother concerning him: "I am on such an intimate footing with Monseigneur that it would be painful in the extreme for me not to express my devotion to him." And it may be said that gratitude caused the spontaneous birth within the Master's heart of the most moving inspirations of his last period.

We are now in 1818, at the moment when the critics of the "Allgemeine musikalische Zeitung," wrote,* with their invariable perspicacity: "Beethoven is now occupied only by bagatelles; he seems to have become entirely unable to

---

* An exception must be made in the case of the celebrated critic *and musician* Hoffmann, whose intelligent sympathy won from Beethoven the compliment "that it had done him a world of good."

write great works." But he will take it upon himself "to reassure his friends as to his mental condition." For some time he has been seen to shut himself up in the archduke's library, that unique collection of early music * to whose enrichment he himself had contributed from the Birkenstock foundation; he passes whole hours poring over the Palestrina motets, either copied in score or in the books of the Gregorian offices. Is Beethoven aiming to become a chanter? Assuredly — a chanter of God's praises.

"To write true sacred music," he jots down, "consult the chorales of the monks, study the ancient psalms and the Catholic chants in their veritable prosody." And to the archduke he writes: "The essential point is to obtain a fusion of styles, a matter wherein the ancients may do us twofold service, having had, for the most part, a real artistic value (as to genius, only the German Händel and Sebastian Bach had that); and if we moderns are not yet so far advanced as our ancestors in point of solidity, the refinement of manners has nevertheless broadened our vision in certain directions." And this idea of a broadened tradition takes shape in the work which is to be the Mass in *D*.

Beethoven, having learned that the archduke was to be installed as Archbishop of Olmütz on March the 9th, 1820, made up his mind to offer him, on that occasion, the fruit of his prolonged meditation on the Divine Sacrifice. But four years are to pass ere the task is accomplished; four years of poverty, during which "he immolates before his art all the miseries of daily existence." — "Oh, God above all," he writes, "for Providence knows why it dispenses joys and

* At present the property of the Vienna Conservatory.

woes to men." And, of a truth, God permitted that the pledge of friendship should become a source of profit to the great man. All the courts of Europe were invited to subscribe to a manuscript copy of the Mass. Of ten copies subscribed for, three were taken by musicians, princes Radziwill and Galitzin and the members of the Saint Cecilia Society of Frankfort. The king of France acted very handsomely; he sent the fifty ducats for the subscription (taken from his "Menus Plaisirs") together with a gold medal bearing his likeness and the engraved words "Le Roi à M. Beethoven," accompanied by a flattering letter.* Beethoven, very proud of this testimonial, had an engraving made from it which he kept in his room; and he charged his friend Bernard to publish in his paper "how this affair had shown him a prince of generous and delicate feeling."

Why did he not ask any subscription whatever from the Austrian court? Because at that time his friends, headed by Count Lichnowsky and the Archduke, had persuaded him to write a mass especially for the Emperor. In fact, they took advantage of the festivals in honor of the imperial

---

* With respect to this letter an error should be corrected which has been made unanimously by Beethoven's biographers, both German and French. The most recent one, Dr. Riemann, himself committed it in his last publication of Thayer's works. They have it that the royal letter was signed by a certain Gentleman of the chamber, *Ferdinand d'Achâlz*, or *d'Achâle* — a personage totally unknown to the history of the French *Chancellerie*. To avoid this blunder, however, it would have been necessary merely to examine the original document, at the foot of which the signature *Le duc de la Châtre* is very legibly displayed in good French characters. Which shows that history written from hearsay or from compilations runs the risk of not being invariably exact.

family to produce one of his overtures, at the Josephstadt Theatre, and to revive *Fidelio* at the Kärnthnerthor Theatre, in hopes that, by favor of these manifestations of loyalty, they might obtain for their protégé the position rendered vacant by the death of Teyber, the Court Composer. Count Dietrichstein, Court Intendant of Music, took the matter in hand. Franz II, whose minister of finance had just authorized the importation, duty free, of an English piano intended for Beethoven, might, through his friendship for the Archduke, have consented to accept a deaf man as his Kapellmeister, had it not been for the precarious state of the Austrian finances. But Teyber was not replaced. Nor should this be looked upon as a crime in the sovereign who, after Austerlitz, banished the desserts from all the tables of the imperial family to devote a few florins more to the country's defense. Only after long hesitation was Beethoven informed of this new mishap. The Emperor's Mass was to remain unfinished. Moreover, Beethoven was in the throes of the bringing forth of another masterwork, the Ninth Symphony, which he destined for his friends of the Philharmonic Society in London. And everything irritated him. He left one villa because its proprietor, Baron Pronay, saluted him politely every time he went out; he ran about bareheaded in a tempest, oblivious of dinnertime or even of bedtime; he was taken for a vagabond and haled to the police-station. — At last the colossus emerges, in full panoply, from the brain of Jupiter; and behold! Jupiter again wears a smiling face. This time the Viennese, despite the vogue of Rossini, prepare an unprecedented triumph for him. First, the address of the Thirty; then, the unselfish zeal of the artists, who refuse their fees for rehearsals — "Whatever you will, for Beethoven!'' — then, despite the terrible vocal difficulties which he obstinately refuses to modify, the enthusiasm of his soloists, of the famous Sontag, of Caroline Unger, and of Preisinger, too, who knew all his symphonies by heart. Then, finally, the unforgettable days of the 7th and 23d of May, 1824, when surging multitudes acclaim the Master, who, alas! no longer could hear them. In the streets of Vienna, everybody salutes him; publishers fight for his works; the announcement of a new quartet suffices to fill a hall; the leading violinists of the time, Bohm, Mayseder, dispute the honor of playing in one of those numerous restaurants in the Prater where musical clocks play the overture to *Fidelio*.

His summer residence becomes a shrine of pilgrimage for a stream of visitors from every quarter. But not all who would like to, obtain audience of the old lion in his lair; for that a *visé* from his Major-domo, Lieutenant-General Steiner, and his Adjutant, little Tobias Hasslinger, is needful. And Generalissimus Beethoven reserves the final decision for himself. These facetious sobriquets he uses to designate the proprietors of the publishing house in Pater Noster Street, his stopping-place and letter-box at Vienna during his vacations.

Picture to yourself this alleyway, a few steps off the Graben. It is four o'clock; the sun is sinking. On the sidewalk are gathered two or three score young artists, composers for the most part, for lack of room in the small music-shop. They are on the lookout for Beethoven's weekly visit. And there, at the turning of the street, appears a short, thickset man of surly mien, with keen eyes beneath iron-gray brows, and bushy hair escaping from under the broad brim of a gray "stovepipe." With his brick-red complexion, his white tie, his collar whose points prodded his cheeks, his long, light-blue overcoat reaching to his ankles and with pockets distended by papers and ear-trumpets, with his erratic double eye-glasses and his gesticulatory gait, we have that legendary figure which provoked the wild laughter of the Viennese street-urchins and made Frau von Breuning exclaim, "I really don't dare take a walk with him!" — But for all that, it sets their hearts throbbing, and ears are strained to catch the replies to the strange monologue that forms his conversation with Steiner.

In spite of an exterior so little prepossessing, the Master always gave young composers a kind reception: "I haven't much time, but show me something."*

And, beneath the ruddy bunches of grapes in the vaulted wine-cellars where he loved to drink with visitors, Beethoven will meet Rossini, whose ignorance he makes fun of while admiring his *Barbier;* Weber, in whom he will greet the creator of German Opera: "Devil of a fellow! Lucky dog!" (so he characterizes the author of *Euryanthe);* then F. Wieck, the future father-in-law of Schumann, who will prevail on him to give a last improvisation on a ramshackle piano; Schubert, who has sold his books to obtain a hearing of *Fidelio,* and in whom Beethoven recognizes the divine spark; Freudenberg, the organist, whose thoughts are centered on Palestrina and church music; the harp-maker Stumpff, to whom he makes this prediction, "Bach will live again when he is studied again;" — and many others.

* These are the very words with which we were welcomed, fifty years later, by our master César Franck.

LUDWIG VAN BEETHOVEN

To everybody he appears jovial, full of whimsies, musical or otherwise; when he criticizes politics, the emperor, the cookery, the French, the taste of the Viennese, it is without bitterness, and, as Rochlitz says, "Everything ends with a *bon mot.*"

At this particular time he is overflowing with delight at his commission from Prince Galitzin to compose three quartets, the compensation for which will insure him his daily bread — though the great Russian nobleman, stricken by a succession of reverses, was unfortunately unable to pay at the time expected. "If I were not simply at the end of my resources, I should write nothing but symphonies and church music, or at most quartets," is his answer to his publishers, his brother and the friends who urge him to compose an opera, "the only kind of work that pays." He is assailed by a host of literary folk, poets, poetesses, librettists — Grillparzer, Sporschill, *Frau Major* Neumann. They go so far as to suggest his writing an overture for the synagogue: "That would be the limit!" declares nephew Carl. But Beethoven does not listen to them. His thoughts are elsewhere.

What good are romantic books like *Melusine,* or insipid historical adventures? Is it not the artist's end to serve in his own way, to show man engaged in the eternal conflict between good and evil? To "The Victory of the Cross," an oratorio whose subject pleased him, but which Bernard's allegories had disfigured, he preferred the poem of "Saul and David," where the same idea is treated more simply, more synthetically. We know through Holz, whose caustic wit had obtained him a certain influence over the Master at Schindler's expense, that he had the entire plan of it mapped out in his head. A double chorus, after the fashion of Greek tragedy, was now to take part in the action, and anon to serve as a commentary; and the employment of two ancient Gregorian modes would have shown musicians a new path.

Alas! the oratorio, along with the Requiem or the Te Deum he projected after hearing a High Mass at St. Charles's, was destined to remain unachieved. After so many raptures, this crowning joy was not to be tasted by Beethoven.

Following a sojourn at the home of his brother, the ex-druggist,who entertained him with the greatest cordiality at his new place, Wasserhof, Beethoven on his return to Vienna was seized with a violent cold, and took to his bed. He was never to rise again.

Farewell to plans of a journey to the land of Palestrina, and to that Provence "where the women wear the shape of Venus, and speak so sweetly." Farewell to the English Pactolus; farewell to the dream of a "serene old age in the bosom of some little Court, where one could write for the glory of the Almighty," before going to rest "like a child grown old" among the portraits of the masters one has loved. — Beethoven was not to have "room of his own," a modest house such as he had wished for. He even had to give up the plans he had made for Carl's future. His nephew at this time is a simple cadet in the Eighth Infantry regiment at Iglau, and Beethoven writes: "All my hopes are vanishing, of having beside me a being in whom I might see my better self reanimate."

Nevertheless, his confidence in God remains unshaken: "Some one will surely be at hand to close my eyes." And Providence puts the little von Breuning in his path. Is it his own youth that he rediscovers in this pretty child's features?

One would say so; for almost at the same time, in a letter
from his old friends Wegeler and Eleonore, there come, like
a breath of his native air, some of those recollections of Bonn
that are ever-present in his heart: "I still keep the paper
silhouette of your Lorchen!" In thought he journeys to
"the lovely scenes where first he saw the day." And that
humming in his ears, is it not the sound of the bells in the
Minorite church where, a mere lad, he took the measure of
the pedals in drawings found among his papers after death?
And the color of the sparkling wine sent him from Mayence
— does it not recall the brightness of the sunny banks of
"Father Rhine"? And his grandfather's portrait, that he
rescued from the paternal heritage — how he now recognizes
himself therein, with what satisfaction he contemplates it!

Then it was (so Lenz informs us) that his friends noted
the disappearance of the famous theist inscription from the
Egyptian temple. And what replaces it at his bedside? "The
Imitation of Christ."

He is found reading Forkel's Life of Bach, and under-
scoring passages in it. On his bed he is occupied, with in-
fantile delight, in turning the leaves of the magnificent Händel
edition which Stumpff has just presented to him; or, it may
be, of the collection of Schubert's last songs. He regales
himself on delicacies brought by friends; — the soup of Frau
von Breuning, the preserves of Pasqualati, even the iced
punch permitted by Dr. Malfatti, who is now reconciliated,
and more indulgent than the others to the sick man's vaga-
ries, allow him to forget for a moment the "seventy-five
phials of medicaments, not counting the powders," the aro-
matic steam-baths and the repeated tappings from which
relief is vainly expected. He still finds a way to launch his

habitual sallies at the learned gentlemen of the Faculty: "Plaudite, amici, comœdia finita est," he says* when, after a long consultation, he sees them turn away.

Finally, he extols the Philharmonic, whose princely gift of one hundred pounds sterling dissipates his last anxieties concerning money; and he himself paraphrases the Händel chorus: "If any doctor can still help me, his name shall be called wonderful." So he is not surprised when his physician informs him that the moment has arrived when he should perform the last rites of a Christian. Here Wawruch may speak: "He read my message with admirable serenity, slowly and thoughtfully; his face shone as if transfigured; pressing my hand warmly and earnestly, he said, 'Let the Herr Pfarrer be called;' and, with a friendly smile, 'I shall see you again soon.' Then he relapsed into silence and meditation."

Of a truth, a moving sight — the author of the Mass in *D* thus setting the world an example of a Christian death. Schindler, Gerhard von Breuning, and Frau van Beethoven, saw the sick man fold his hands and receive, with edifying fervor, the viaticum and extreme unction. "I thank you, reverend father, you have brought me consolation," he said thereafter; then he explained his last wishes to Schindler.

We know of the terrible agony; of the broken exclamations "Do you hear the bell?" — "Now the scene changes!" — of his death amid the crash of thunder and a tempest of hail.

* V. Wilder and some other biographers set the time of this utterance after his reception of the last sacraments. It is now proved beyond doubt that such a transposition is an historical error. *Cf.* in Thayer, Vol. V, pp. 485–490, the last word of German criticism on this subject.

A few months later, in this *Schwarzspanierhaus* still saturated with the sublime inspirations of the last quartets, the Viennese publishers met in eager competition for the manuscripts of Beethoven — for a few paltry florins. The auctioneer's hammer fell on priceless relics: "Are you all done? — Sold!"

VI

HIS MUSIC

THIRD PERIOD: REFLECTION

One curious particular deserving of mention is the suddenness of the transformations of style in the *processus* of Beethoven's art. There are, so to speak, no transitions; and pieces presaging the sudden imminent change from one style to the other, are rare indeed.

While the second manner, that of expression, moves in a totally different sphere from the first, and may scarcely be divined in the *Largo* of Op. 10, the passage from this second epoch to the third is yet more sharply marked. In spirit there is hardly anything in common between the sonatas Op. 101 and 102, which begin this last period, and similar, even advanced, works of the one preceding — Op. 81 and 90, for instance. One solitary inspiration of tender and absolute beauty, a moving proof of sympathy for a great sorrow, the *Elegischer Gesang* for four voices and stringed instruments on the death of Baroness Pasqualati, already bears a presentiment of the religious effusions of the Mass in *D*.

What change can have come over Beethoven's spiritual state to render his creative style all of a sudden (from 1815) so different from what it was in 1814? To what event may this sudden transformation be attributed? — In vain shall we try to attach this new style to any *external* cause whatever. The source of the evolution of present interest should be sought only in the soul of the poet; it was from his heart that poured those vivifying floods which refresh all other hearts athirst for the Ideal. No longer, as in the second

BEETHOVEN IN 1824
Pencil sketch by Stephen Decker

period, do we witness an exteriorization of emotions, but, on the contrary, the altogether *internal* travail of a thought of genius acting on itself, within a soul closed against outside turmoil and agitation.

For this reason we have termed these last twelve years in our hero's career the period of *reflection*.

Let us try to define, briefly, Beethoven's moral situation at this conjuncture. — He has reached his forty-fifth year without having found that feminine soul which might have brought into his life of isolation all the sweetness of conjugal and family affection. All the women whose companionship for life he desired, are married. Though Giulietta, Countess von Gallenberg, attempts one day to revive their friendship, it is because, goaded by adversity, she seeks pecuniary assistance for her husband: "He was always my enemy, and that is precisely the reason that I shall do him all the good I can!" Amalie Sebald is the wife of a Councillor of State, and Therese Malfatti is engaged to Baron Drosdick, whom she will marry the year following. Beethoven has abandoned the useless pursuit of that "mutual love" which he so often has sung; — he has renounced love.

Should it still ever happen that he casts his eyes on a being of the opposite sex — if he writes: "Love alone can make life happy. O God! Let me at last find her who shall confirm me in virtue, and shall be mine!" — all this is but the final flickering of a flame near to going out, the last leaf of a book about to be closed for ever, and whose closing he will seal with the two beautiful vocal poems "To the Distant Beloved" and "Resignation." After the year of the Vienna Congress, so full of glory for him, he is still left without an official position. His reduced annuity barely suffices for his needs and more especially for the expenses of Carl, that nephew so unsatisfactory in almost every respect. Besides this, his deafness has now become total (the innumerable ear-trumpets from Maelzel are of but the slightest use), and forbids not only all connected intercourse with his fellows, but even the most elementary functions of his art. Isolated in everything, without wife, without sweetheart, with neither position nor resources, even deprived of hearing his own music, his existence may well be termed a living death.

What does Beethoven, withal? — Far from resigning himself to despair, and wishing to have done with a wretched existence which no longer offers him a single exterior attraction, he turns his gaze inward, to that soul which he has ever striven to raise toward God, the Source of all that is good and beautiful. "Yes," he said to Stumpff in 1824, "he who would touch the heart must seek his inspiration on high. Otherwise, there will be nothing but notes — a body without soul — will there not? And what is a body without a soul? Mere dust, a little mud, is it not? — The spirit should make itself free from matter, in which for a time the divine spark is imprisoned. Like the furrow to which the laborer confides the precious seed, his part is to make it germinate and bring forth abundant fruit; and, multiplied thus, the spirit will strive to ascend to the source whence it sprang. For it is only at the cost of unremitting endeavor that it can employ the forces placed at its disposal, and that the creature may render homage to the Creator and Preserver of infinite Nature."

And thus he comes to lead a purely introspective life, an almost monastic life, contemplative, intense, fruitful. He no longer creates with an eye to ephemeral success, as in his youth, or to find a vent for the expression of his impressions, his feelings, his passions, as in the second period; he creates in the fullness of joy or in the fullness of grief, with the sole aim of elevating and purifying that soul wherein he now lives — alone.

This is the true cause of that change in style to which we owe the Mass and the Ninth Symphony.

After the Congress of Vienna we observe, not without surprise, a sort of fallow season in the productivity of this fecund genius. The *Allgemeine musikalische Zeitung* is not altogether in the wrong — he composes but little: only two sonatas for the entire year of 1815, a single one in 1816; in 1818, nothing but a few *Lieder* and a sketch for string-quintet. What can be the matter? — One might allege the anxieties attendant on his nephew's education, his interminable law-suits, the legal memorials which he insists on drawing up himself. But have we not ascertained that neither travel, nor the thousand details of external existence, nor love itself in the very paroxysm of passion, had hitherto succeeded in checking the exuberant flow of production in Beethoven? The real reason for this silence is, that during these three years in which he finds himself, as it were, forced to live within himself, Beethoven has *reflected*. Richard Wagner will do the same at the dawn of his Third Manner. And the result of this prolonged reflection will be, that the author of the sonata Op. 57, of the seventh quartet, of the Sixth Symphony, then — and not until then — feels that he *knows how to compose!*

This he declares at various times; for example, apropos of Op. 106: "What I write now does not resemble what I did formerly; it is *a little better.*" To Potter, an Englishman who spoke to him at Nussdorf in 1817 about the astounding success of the septet, Beethoven replies: "At that time I understood nothing of composition; now I *know how to compose!*"

To compose?!

How many people are there in France — since we, in our Latin country, have abandoned Latinistic studies — who are capable of giving an exact definition of this term?   Most assuredly, the majority of those who are called "composers" would be quite as incapable of doing so as our primary pupils.

Compose, *componere* — to put together, to join into one whole, to arrange side by side; that is the material, fundamental meaning of the word.   But the Latins attached to this noble vocable another, more abstract sense, containing an idea of comparison, of regular succession, of proportion and order:

Si parva licet componere magnis,

which importantly modifies its primary signification.   And solely in this latter acceptation should it be applied to a work of art.

We do not consider that we shall stray from our subject if we examine the divers phases of this creative labor.   By so doing we shall enter more intimately into our hero's thought; we shall unveil — so far as such a thing is possible — the mystery of his artistic creative spirit.

In everything human — in art above all else — we distinguish between *matter* and *form*.   Now, to shape the musical material and so arrange it as to *set it in action,* is not that the whole secret of composition?

In music, the principal agent of the work is what we call the *theme,* or *idea.*   It may be defined as follows: The musical *idea* is constituted from sonorous elements furnished by the *imagination*, selected by the *heart*, ordered by the *intelligence*.

It would take too long to enter into details; but we must conclude that if the *unaided* intelligence can bring forth only productions which are inevitably cold and — to be brief — useless, since they are not vivified by the instinctive spark of genius; — on the other hand, instinct *by itself* is wholly incapable of building up a work, and, without the aid of intelligence, can gropingly create nothing better than ingenious, but always ephemeral, improvisations. Nor can these two faculties united suffice to create a beautiful work if sentiment, emotion, the *heart*, in a word, does not supervene to choose the expressive elements and thus to animate the superb, but rigid, statue by endowing it with speech and motion by virtue of its divine lifebreath.

Let no one think that what we have just explained represents a *system* of composition — *e.g.*, that peculiar to Beethoven — and that no others can exist. No; this process is *composition itself*, and, while different artists differ in the details, all the geniuses (all those, at least, into whose work we have been permitted to gain a clear insight) have never proceeded otherwise. Carl von Dittersdorf (1739-1799), a composer of the second rank, perhaps, yet very interesting by reason of his culture and intelligence, gives an excellent summing up, in his Memoirs, of what we affirm above: "I had reached the conclusion," he writes, "that a composer, besides a great deal of taste, imagination, fantasy, and technical knowledge, needs, above all, creative genius. Now, this last, although it be a gift of nature, cannot conquer appreciation until the musician has acquired sufficient culture. In the contrary case, his genius develops like a wild plant, ·without order, without æsthetic power, without beauty."

Such was also Beethoven's opinion. He likewise expressed the view that the acquisition of that "sufficient culture" whereof Dittersdorf speaks can result only from prolonged preliminary labors most conscientiously carried out. Consequently, he considers this necessary work something wholly distinct from the study of composition properly so called. "To become a composer," he said, "one must first have studied harmony and counterpoint during a period of from seven to eleven years, so as to accustom one's self to bend the inventive faculty to the rules, whenever imagination and feeling shall awaken." To Dr. Pachler, who gave him a manuscript for examination, the Master. responded that "it was very good for any one who had never learned to compose, but that after a more thorough study of composition the author would be enabled to perceive its numerous defects."

And so it came, that after more than twenty years of a career replete with masterworks, Beethoven could say, at the beginning of his forty-seventh year, "Now, I KNOW HOW TO COMPOSE!"

How is this *reflective* frame of mind which we have ascertained in Beethoven, and which has just ripened to the conclusion that he "knows how to compose," going to express itself in music? — It will be through a manifest and intentional return to the old *traditional forms*. Do not misinterpret the meaning of these words, a *return to tradition*. We should never think of maintaining that Beethoven returns, in full maturity, to a servile imitation of the musical types employed

[96]

by his predecessors or contemporaries. But what may be asserted is, that the entire æsthetics of his third manner are founded on ancient forms theretofore unemployed by him — forms whose noble and generous atavism endows the most venturesome compositions with a wholesome and robust temperament, a solid ancestral basis. And it is precisely his novel, "broadened" (as Beethoven himself said) employment of these traditional elements which imparts to the works of this period their profound and incontestable originality.

These forms are the *Fugue*, the *Suite*, the *Chorale with Variations*.

Brought up from youth in the greatest admiration and most sincere respect for J. S. Bach, so much so that in 1800 he took the initiative, so to speak, in making a collection for the benefit of Regina Bach, the last daughter of the illustrious Cantor, and that on April the 22d of the following year he was among the first to subscribe to an edition of the works of Bach, the author of the Mass in *B* minor; and, on the other hand, full of reverence for Händel; — Beethoven had not attempted the fugue-form save on rare occasions and with no novelty whatever in the result. During the two earlier periods his fugues were nothing but unimportant exercises for him, "musical skeletons" (for instance, the rather uninteresting fugue in the ninth quartet, and the one in the Variations on a Theme from the ballet *Prometheus*), or merely one other means of development (Third and Seventh Symphonies). Beginning with 1815, everything changes in this respect; he sees in the fugue an *end*, rather than a technical *means*. Far more; in contact with his genius this form, so frequently cold and pulseless with musicians antedating Bach, becomes eminently expressive. "Into the old mould handed down to us, we must pour an element of genuine poetry." In his hands the fugue-form, like the sonata-form, is now to express his inmost feelings — peaceful, sorrowful, joyful.

Beethoven's fugues, in general, are perfectly regular, agreeing in construction with the traditional architecture. We even encounter artifices of combination (subjects in diminution, in changed rhythm, in contrary motion, etc.) more frequently than in similar pieces from the end of the eighteenth century; but what differentiates them especially from these latter is their *musical nature*, which is *Beethoven*, and not Bach or somebody else. Could this be otherwise? Is not this precisely what constitutes the strength of the traditional forms? Without being essentially altered in their arrangement, which is founded on logic and beauty, they readily yield themselves to the *individual* moulding of geniuses differing greatly in type, for the production of new masterworks; whereas in the hands of mediocrity they remain stubbornly intractable.

Beethoven's fugues differ in an equal degree, as music, from Bach's, as these latter differ from those of Pasquini or Frescobaldi — and nevertheless they are all *fugues*.

This form, treated *for its own sake*, often occurs in the Beethoven of the third period, more particularly in the following works:

Sonata for violoncello, Op. 102, No. 2 (1815); Fugue for string-quintet, Op. 137 (1817); Sonatas for piano, Op. 106 (1818) and Op. 110 (1821); Variations on a waltz by Diabelli, Op. 120; Overture "zur Weihe des Hauses," Op. 121 (1822); Missa solemnis (1818–1822); grand Fugue for string-quartet, Op. 133 (1825); fourteenth Quartet, in *C*♯, Op. 131 (1826);

without counting the numerous pieces whose construction is influenced by the fugue-principle.

The same is true of the Suite-form, which had been neglected for many years, and which Beethoven revived in his last quartets.

But it is, above all, the oldentime Chorale with Variations which reappears in this last manner. It reappears in the Beethoven of 1824 in the same spirit as in the Bach of 1702; the Bach who, while magnifying the essays of Pachelbel and Buxtehude, created the amplificative variation.* As we have observed in the fugue, the *music* lends to Beethoven's variations such a different aspect from those by Bach, that persons of superficial judgment would fail, in most instances, to discern the analogy.

This species of variation, sometimes so *amplifying* the theme as to make an entirely new melody spring out of it (twelfth quartet), and again so *simplifying* it as to reduce it almost to melodic immobility (fourteenth quartet), is not met with until the year 1820, in the Adagio of the sonata Op. 109; but thereafter (and most abundantly) in Op. 111, in his very curious commentaries on the insipid waltz by Diabelli (1823), and finally in the last string-quartets. So it might be said that this wholly novel adaptation of a very old form was the last, and not the least sublime, manifestation of Beethoven's genius.

Hence, it was by leaning on the traditional forms and identifying them with his internal conception that this pretended revolutionary was able to contribute so powerfully to the progress of his art. And here we take the word "progress" in its etymological signification, *progressus*, the going

* Chorales for organ, of 1702, 1720 and 1750.

forward in the sane and safe path already opened by great predecessors, — and not in the sense which seems nowadays to be generally attached to it, the seeking after novelty at all hazards by means quite divested of logic or harmony. "The new, the original," said Beethoven, "springs up by itself, without our taking thought."

All the productions of this admirable period ought to be examined in detail. To lovers of art, their study offers the assurance of ineffable delights. For lack of space, we shall dwell on only a few works, limiting ourselves to indicating the special character of each of the others. But before taking up this examination it is necessary to elucidate a spiritual state which, making itself felt (so to speak) throughout the second period of the author of the Ninth Symphony, assumed, in the course of the third period, such importance that it might have served as the point of departure for a new transformation, a fourth style, had not death come prematurely to cut short a career already so complete.

It is the religious sentiment of which we desire to speak.

A Catholic by race and education, Beethoven remained, in his life and in his works, a believer. He believed in a God who enjoins us to "love one another," to "forgive those who trespass against us"; in a God whom he "had not ceased to serve from his youth up," in a Judge "before whom he would not fear to appear at the last day."

Did the poet who, in his last symphony, could write such a beautiful vindication of Charity, put his religion into practice? A delicate question to approach. Some have thought it possible to do so without the support of documentary evidence. What we possess proofs of is, that he fasted on Fridays and on the eve of festivals; that he held morning and evening prayers with his nephew, and insisted that the latter should learn the catechism, "for it is only on this foundation that a man can be raised up."

What appears unequivocally, both in his writings and his compositions, is a growingly accentuated tendency towards purely religious music. To the worship of God in nature there succeeded, in Beethoven, the longing for God for God's own sake; and, as we have seen, it was the "Imitation of Christ" which took the place of Sturm's books on his table and among familiar objects.

Let us recall his efforts to assimilate the art of the old masters of the centuries of Faith undiluted, and his resolution to "write nothing but religious music;" we shall be able to arrive at the conviction that this resolution was no vain phrase.

On arranging according to species and date the works of the period we have now reached, as we did those of the second period, it will be evident that from 1818 onward, after the "fallow season" of which we spoke above, his pianistic productivity, almost entirely neglected during ten years, revives to a puissant fecundity in masterworks. One might say that, wearied with the powerful, tender or picturesque sonorities of instrumental collectivity, Beethoven thenceforward cared solely for self-communion in the most intimate forms of music.

From 1818 to 1822 there are four grand sonatas, eighteen curious bagatelles (Op. 119 and 126), the rondo on "the lost Groschen" (Op. 129), and, like a *jeu d'esprit* amidst the elaboration of two wellnigh superhuman works, the thirty-two variations (Op. 120).

All the while, though writing for the *Hammerclavier*, his mind was busied with "the most finished of his productions," the *Missa solemnis*, the preparatory work on which extends through these four years. And then, almost immediately, comes the Ninth Symphony.

But after these two tremendous flights toward the Divine Love and the love of mankind in God, Beethoven returns to his reflections. Without disclosing the secret to us — however we may sometimes suspect it — he sings within himself what he has just been singing for others, and, readopting this form of chamber music so long slighted, he breathes all his soul into the last five quartets.

It being impossible here to analyze this legion of masterpieces, we shall not try to follow a chronological arrangement, as we have done till now, in order that we may finish our essay worthily with those two sublime works, the Choral Symphony and the Missa solemnis.

The Sonatas

Let us pass over, regretfully, the charming sonata Op. 101, which Beethoven dedicated to his friend Baroness Ertmann — a work in which the fugue enters for the first time into the ·sonata-form; over the two sonatas for piano and violoncello, Op. 102, even though the introduction of the one and the Adagio of the other may be reckoned among the loftiest melodic inspirations of the Master. We begin with the year 1818. Imagine the poor great man forced, by the needs of daily existence, to incessant production. Obliged to appease the rapacity of his publishers, he devotes night-hours to writing pot-boilers — an Andante for piano; Six Themes with variations, for flute, Op. 105; Ten Russian, Scotch and Tyrolese Songs with variations, for piano and flute, Op. 107; Twelve Bagatelles, Op. 119; a Rondo, Op. 129; and Six Bagatelles, Op. 126.

The forthbringing of Opus 106 comes to brighten these troublous times. One must have suffered one's self to dare attempt the execution of the Adagio in $F\sharp$ minor, of such intense emotional power, and hovering between the gloomiest resignation and the most radiant hopefulness! Aside from the fugue serving as finale — a strange fugue, unrestful, with a dash of blue sky amidst the clouds, but producing an over-whelming effect when the interpretation is worthy of the music — aside from this fugue, the entire sonata is built up in a fashion wholly traditional, and, in spite of that (perhaps because of it), it presents itself, through the choice of ideas and nobility of construction, in immeasurable grandeur.

Without pausing for the pretty sonata in E (Op. 109), in two movements, we shall take up Op. 110, one of the most moving compositions of the third period.

Almost all Beethoven's works (at least, the important ones) bear, as we know, significant dedications; Opus 110 alone has none. Should we feel surprise at this? Could Beethoven dedicate to any one but himself this expression in music of an internal convulsion in his life? Triumphing for the moment over the first attacks of the malady to which he was to succumb six years later; triumphing also, through his recent winning of a lawsuit, over grievous family cares — worse sufferings for him than the sickness itself; exulting in the serene joy of work on the Mass, he sought to transcribe in music the moral drama in which he had been the chief actor. Four years thereafter he will put forth a complement

[103]

of like nature to this sonata: the fifteenth quartet. But, whereas the quartet, almost in its entirety, is a religious burst of gratitude to God, the vanquisher of evil, the sonata carries us into the very midst of a crisis; it resembles a cruel and desperate conflict with this Evil, the principle of annihilation, followed by a return to Life celebrated by a hymn of triumphant jubiliation. This work might be likened to Op. 57, constructed on nearly the same plan; but in our present sonata in A♭ the reascension towards the light is treated in a far more moving and dramatic fashion.

At the outset of the first movement Beethoven presents, as the second element in the initial idea, that theme from Haydn which he treated so often. And here this theme, the last tribute of the aging Master to the teacher who guided his first steps in composition, seems like a symbol of moral and physical health; likewise the direction *con amabilità* instructs us concerning the manner of its interpretation. After a Scherzo whose restlessness already intrudes on the *amiable* calm of the first movement, a Recitative intervenes, alternating with ritornelli in orchestral style. We have previously encountered this form of declamation without words (sonata Op. 31, No. 2), and shall meet with it again in the last quartets and the Ninth Symphony. Now there arises, in the key of A♭ minor, one of the most poignant expressions of grief conceivable to man. Too soon the phrase dies away. It makes way for the fugue in A♭ (major), whose subject is derived from the *amiable* theme of the first movement. It might be termed an effort of will to shake off suffering. But the latter is the stronger. And the grief-stricken phrase is repeated, this time in *G* minor. This reappearance in a tonality so distant and strange, transporting us into a *place* so different from that wherein the rest of the sonata takes its way, has the effect of bringing us face to face with the final throes of an implacable moral agony. But now Will asserts itself against the forces of annihilation, and a dynamic succession of tonic chords ushers in the key of *G* major, in which the fugue resumes its progress, though presented in *contrary motion:* It is the resurrection!

And here it is impossible to misunderstand the author's intentions when he writes, at the head of this new appearance of the health-motive reversed, the direction "Poi a poi di nuovo vivente"; whereas the second arioso is marked "Perdendo le forze." Yes, strength revives according as we approach the *place* where health was transmuted into music, that is to say, the initial key. Finally, as a conclusion, a song of thanksgiving enters in victorious amplification of the melodic phrase, triumphantly closing this work, which will remain a type of eternal beauty. — Opus 110 was dated "on Christmas-Day of the year 1821."

Sonata Op. 11, the last great work in sonata-form for piano, is divided into two parts; the first very regular, in first-movement form, with two themes strongly contrasted in character; the second, entitled Arietta (in the rather unusual time of 9-16), bringing in four superb variations and an important final development.

The Quartets

Incontestably, it is in the last quartets and the Missa solemnis that Beethoven's genius manifests itself in the newest and most untrammeled fashion. Therefore, while the entire *second manner* was doing service in the repertories of orchestral and chamber-music concerts, the works in question remained for a long time — a very long time — not understood, or, even worse, misunderstood. Their artistic scope still overpasses our twentieth century.

We shall, none the less, venture an attempt to examine their musical significance; so far, at least, as our feeble comprehension has succeeded in divining it.

TWELFTH QUARTET, Op. 127, composed in 1824. — The first movement, through the uniformity of its rhythm and the interprenetration of one theme by the other, appears, precisely by virtue of its monorhythmic structure, to withdraw itself from the habitual scheme of the sonata. Such is not the case; the theme of the Introduction is at hand to furnish the *contrasting* influence requisite to this form of composition. Hence, far from remaining, as in the preceding works, a passive prelude, the introduction now plays a rôle of prime importance in the construction of the piece; for it is this introduction which, by its triple appearance, regulates the tonal architectural scheme $E\flat - G - C$. The melody constituting the theme of the Adagio is so radiant in splendor that on reading it one feels himself at once transported with joy and bewildered with admiration. This melody is an echo, almost a reminiscence, of the *Benedictus qui venit* of the Mass in *D*, but here, it must be acknowledged, with a far greater intensity of expression. It would seem that Beethoven, in this theme of fivefold variation, intended to expound, after the manner of the Church Fathers, by an admirable commentary, the nature of this "blessed is he that cometh in the name of the Lord." The change of *place* and *person* in the third variation, although the *principle* remains immovable, tends, in our opinion, to confirm this hypothesis,

[106]

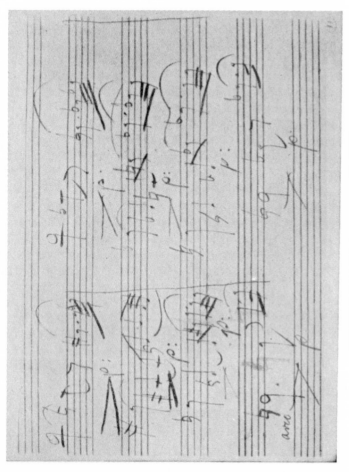

AUTOGRAPH FROM THE QUARTET, NO. 13 (1825)

(From the collection of M. Ch. Malherbe)

evoking a sensible and musical image of the *incarnation* of this "blessed one." However it may be, this Adagio will endure as the most sublime of prayers. With the Scherzo and the Finale we are brought back to earth, and again meet the Beethoven of the second period; the Finale would re-awaken the pastoral impressions of 1808, did not the development of the dream which ends it, elevating the almost trivial phrase of the beginning to incommensurable heights, supervene to remind us that all this is not occurring between Döbling and Kahlenberg, but altogether in the poet's soul.

THIRTEENTH QUARTET, Op. 130, composed in 1825, finished in November, 1826. — First movement: the conflict between two instincts, imploring gentleness and inexorable violence. The longing for gentleness succeeds, after many struggles, in permeating the constitution of the violent theme and subduing it wholly. The Andante, generally misunderstood, even by executants endowed with good intentions, is of great beauty in its predesigned monotony; but one must know how to enter into and interpret the profoundly intimate mood of the second theme. Here Beethoven again takes up a type of Andante which he had employed extensively, and then abandoned for more than twenty years; now he imbues it with fresh youth. The Cavatina is like a memory, faint, yet replete with feeling, of two preceding masterworks. In its general color it recalls the melancholy poetry of the *Elegischer Gesang* (Op. 118), and, in its construction, the grand theme of the Adagio in the Choral Symphony. The Finale is one of the rare pieces built up with three ideas. As in the Heroic Symphony, the third theme enters by a prolonged tone, like a stranger; but, although coming from so distant a country, it finally establishes itself in the same place as the other two themes, by a sort of miracle of construction. This Finale is the last composition finished by Beethoven. It was the Grand Fugue, Op. 133, that the Master had in mind to employ as the peroration to the colossal thirteenth quartet. But, at the instance of his publishers, he resigned himself to have it issued separately. The work is extraordinarily interesting, and one may well ask why no one ever thinks to execute it where it belongs, that is, at the end of the quartet. It is a conflict between two *subjects*, the one mildly melancholy and very closely related to the *key-theme* of the fifteenth quartet, the other infused with the most exuberant gayety. And, besides, it is very beautiful music.

FOURTEENTH QUARTET, Op. 131, composed in 1826. — This deserves attention, because its conception and the form thence evolved are absolutely novel, and exhibit the sonata-type in but one movement out of six. The architecture of these six movements, which are played without a break, is surprising in its marvelous equilibrium, established according to the cadence-formula of the tonality of $C\sharp$ minor.*

A fugue of regular structure, whose subject is almost classic, but whose developments singularly magnify its significance, forms the majestic portal. Then, as though he proposed to present in this quartet an historical review of the ancient forms, Beethoven resuscitates, in charming fashion, the Suite-type in the brisk *D*-major Vivace. After

* For readers who have made a study of harmonic devices we give the formula in detail: (1) Tonic; (2) Subdominant, (3) Relative of the subdominant; (4) Relative; (5) Dominant; (6) Tonic.

an introductory recitative the *A*-major Andante, in dialogue-form, gives out its theme, which engenders seven very curious variations. These latter are disposed in such a way that the theme, during the first half of the piece, seems to be congealing little by little (if such a comparison be permissible) until it gives an impression of complete immobility. Called back to life by a new recitative, it revives as if regretfully, finishing the movement with a few sighs. After a long and joyous Scherzo in *E* major a deeply moving song-phrase in *G*-sharp minor prepares the advent of the triumphant Finale, which appears (at last!) in *first-movement* form, and evokes melodically the subject of the initial fugue.

FIFTEENTH QUARTET, Op. 132, composed in 1825, finished in 1826. — Like Sonata Op. 110, this quartet in its entirety is a musical representation of the dénouement of a crisis — in this case probably physical, since this composition coincides with the illness, sufficiently serious to necessitate a month in bed, which Beethoven passed through from April to August 1825. But, of this crisis, only a memory remains; from the entire work there emanates a sentiment of religious effusion, of tender filial gratitude. The introduction, a short motive of four notes, offers the key without which none may enter into the superb edifice formed by the first movement. To explain how this key turns in the locks to open, one by one, all the rooms of the palace, would trespass on the domain of a course in composition; so we shall content ourselves by mentioning the ravishing second theme in three phrases, after the Beethoven system — a theme whose third phrase combines the rhythm of the initial theme of the sonata with the very striking harmony of the *key-motive* in the introduction. Of a truth, one need only read this first movement to be satisfied that Beethoven *knew how to compose!* — A Scherzo with rustic Trio (the last souvenir of the strolling musician's bagpipe) takes us out with the convalescent on his first rambles, albeit with somewhat vacillating step. And then, it is the "song of one restored to health, addressing his grateful heart to God." We say, "to God," for, if we consider the nature of the music, it would be sovereignly absurd to pretend that this wholly Catholic hymn could be addressed to any particular Esculapius! At this period Beethoven, for the composition of his Mass, has been studying intimately the liturgical melodies, and has attentively read Palestrina's works. It is even beyond doubt that he owes to the masters of vocal counterpoint that (for him) new understanding for polyphonic style which intensifies all his latest works. It is, therefore, no matter for astonishment that this "Song of gratitude *in the Lydian mode*" is based on the sixth Gregorian mode. The piece has the cut of a *Lied* in five sections. First, the hymn is enunciated in five periods separated by instrumental interludes; then an episode enters in which, as in Op. 110, the sick man "feels renewed strength"; second exposition of the hymn, but this time *linearly*, while around this line the orchestral theme, originally unpliable, plays in agitated movement. After another episode of "renewed strength" the hymn is sung for the third time, but now it appears fragmentarily, leaving in the foreground the instrumental theme, which the author wishes to have played "*con intimissimo sentimento.*" This theme thus becomes the real song of the grateful soul, while the melody of the hymn takes flight to higher regions. And it is altogether beautiful! In rude contrast, an almost military march brings us back to earth; and a recitative ushers in the outburst of the Finale, written in the old Rondo-form resuscitated for the occasion. Out of this Finale sprang the entire melodic vein of Mendelssohn; but the phrase of the Titan of Bonn is expressive and touching to the same degree that the ideas of the amiable and correct Berliner — which derive, nevertheless, in their essence, from that phrase — are cold and arid of emotion.

SIXTEENTH QUARTET, Op. 135 (1826). — It is replete with loftiest beauties, notably the Andante-song in *D* flat, an echo of one of the bitterest deceptions of Beethoven, the adoptive father. Still, the work cannot, in our opinion, be compared with the four preceding it; and the enigmatical motto of the finale, "Muss es sein?" does little to enhance its value.

THE LIEDER AND THE CANONS

The purely vocal production of the last period is of far greater interest than that of the other two periods. From 1814 to 1820 there are three memorable songs: *Sehnsucht*, in which may already be noted the process of repetition, or rather of echo, employed in the Andante of the Ninth Symphony and the Cavatina of the thirteenth quartet; *An die Hoffnung*, Op. 94, curiously arranged from a tonal point of view, almost a fragment of a drama (the first page, in *B*♭ minor, seems like a sketch for the introduction to the third act of *Parsifal*); finally, *Resignation*, this genial appeal to the light, one of the most concise and finest melodies by Beethoven. We have already mentioned the interesting

Song-Cycle *An die ferne Geliebte*, wherein one might recognize the point of departure of similar compositions of the romantic epoch. In these Schumann excelled.

Beginning with 1820, or what might be termed Beethoven's discovery of the musical styles antedating the seventeenth century, we find nothing written by him in the way of fugitive vocal music but Canons for from two or three up to six voices.

We know the predilection and delicacy with which the art of canon was cultivated by the old masters, who had a habit of corresponding "canonically," and of proposing to each other enigmas for solution. Beethoven, resuming this usage, discovers himself in these brief fantasies as the man of jovial whimsies whom one might have seen, at four o'clock, drinking his habitual *Schoppen* in a cabaret near the ramparts. The Thirty Canons are, for the most part, "congratulations" (*Gratulationen*, as the modern Germans would say), or more or less drole plays on words. *Gratulire*, the canon for the dinner in 1817; a reconciliation is effected with Maelzel on the theme of the Scherzando in the Eighth Symphony. *Gratuliren*, the canon on the name of Hoffmann, sportively displacing the accent; and the canon on the name of Kuhlau (1825), in which, by a bizarre fancy, are interwoven the four notes spelling the name Bach. There are also satirical canons; in the one which he pompously dedicates to the violoncellist Hauschka, Beethoven enjoins him to write a scale, and so we see, after its second entry, the antecedent run up and down the scale of $E\flat$. There are lively ones, like *Rede, rede, rede, rede;* expressive ones, like that for Spohr (1814): "Brief is sorrow, eternal is joy." And there are some which rise to the level of veritable compositions; for example, the

[112]

one conveying his New Year's greeting to Archduke Rudolph, for January the first, 1820: "Alles Gute! Alles Schöne!" also the fine six-part piece on Goethe's lines, "Edel sei der Mensch, hülfreich und gut" (1823).

After mentioning, by way of reminder, the two cantatas with chorus, "Calm Sea and Prosperous Voyage" (1815), and the one for Lobkowitz (1816), besides a March for military music, an Allegro for orchestra (1822) and (in the same year) the Overture for the inauguration of the suburban theatre in Josephstadt, which is in the old form of prelude and fugue, we shall have passed in review all the works of the third period, reserving the two colossi for the last chapter.

VII

THE NINTH SYMPHONY AND THE MISSA SOLEMNIS

THE NINTH SYMPHONY. — At the present time the Choral Symphony is too well known to require any further attempt at analysis here.* We shall merely endeavor to explain what seems to us to be, according to the music, the true meaning of this work. We have not the least pretensions to infallibility; but, should we deceive ourselves, it will be in good faith, and assuredly, less grossly than those who have sought to discover in it a revolutionary apology for liberty.

First of all be it observed, that *all* the typical themes of the symphony present the arpeggio of the chords of *D* or *B* flat, the two tonal bases of the work; one might, therefore, consider this arpeggio as the real cyclic theme of the Ninth Symphony. The entire work is nothing but a conflict between the various states of this theme, restless and changeable in the first two movements, tranquilized in the Adagio, and definitely fixed in the Finale, where words finally enter to explain its intent.

The first movement, constructed after an impeccable sonata plan, leaves an impression of agitation, of breathless pursuit, almost bordering on despair. The analogy of the theme to that of the storm in the Pastoral Symphony arouses the idea of a tempest, not out of doors, this time, but in the heart of a man; and the mysterious question conveyed in the second theme, here remaining unanswered, seems thus to find a fitting explanation. It is the soul, fallen a prey to

---

* A very interesting commentary on the genesis of the work may be found in Prod'homme's book on "Les Symphonies de Beethoven."

BEETHOVEN MONUMENT AT VIENNA

the cruel tortures of doubt. Then, to escape this torment, the man plunges into the torrent of passions, and the feverish activity of the Scherzo, incessantly changing in rhythm and place, would give expression to this new soul-state. But now, in the Trio, a call is heard, several times repeated, which already foreshadows the "brotherly love" motive in the theme; but it passes on, carried away by the tempestuous gust of passion, and the whirlwind recommences in full force. The movement of this Trio has hitherto been variously executed. Most conductors of orchestra slow down recklessly, and transform it into an amiable *villanella* wholly at variance with the composer's intentions. A mere glance at the original manuscript will dissipate all doubts concerning the movement therein indicated by Beethoven — *prestissimo;* which ought, considering the similarity of the two "times," to continue without change the pace set by the preceding *stringendo.* The third piece, the only one outside of the principal tonality, is a prayer whose apparent tranquillity does not exclude the ardor of vehement desire. The soul insistently demands enlightenment, and divine intervention is now on the point of bringing in the light. The theme of this Adagio, which awakens an echo in the deepest recesses of the heart, is precisely the answer to the question asked at the beginning of the movement; the Sphinx, interrogated, divulges her oracle, which runs: "Let us pray." But this prayer is not to be offered without a struggle; there intervenes a theme, passionate at first, thereafter a call to arms (as in the Agnus Dei of the Mass); natheless the beneficent flood, though twice turned aside, resumes its course and rises, as conqueror of the world, unto the threshold of the temple wherein the mystery of Love is to be celebrated. The lofty and generous motive of the Finale, of which we have already noted a presage in two earlier works,* is still the key-arpeggio, but this time appearing almost bereft of movement, having at last arrived at *conviction*. It appears bound together by a chain of secondary notes, which might be taken to symbolize the fraternal clasp of hands united by the love of mankind. After a double exposition of this theme of "mutual love," an initial variation exhibits the soul departing for warfare against the army of Hate, against the host of those "who do not love." A second variation conjures the battle before our eyes; and a third brings back the victorious soul. And yet, this victory does not suffice. From whom shall come the power to make Love everlasting? At this point there arises a liturgical chant, a psalm constructed on the eighth Gregorian mode (with — possibly — a trifle less delicacy in the use of the tritone than was observed by the monkish composers of the middle ages). "Look upward, ye millions, beyond the stars, and ye shall see your heavenly Father, from whom all love floweth." And the religious melody unites with the theme of love to end in a burst of impassioned rapture.

This, so it seems to us, is what one must see in the Choral Symphony, if it be considered with the eyes of the soul.

How is this monumental work, so absolutely new in conception, constructed from the technical point of view? Does the author, for the expression of things so unusual, impatiently break the ancient moulds, scornfully reject the ancient formulas, trample under foot all the traditions? Not at all! In the whole range of Beethoven's works there is, perhaps, no symphony (save the first two) which departs less from

* See pp. 23 and 71.

the traditional form than this Ninth, monstrous as it appeared to his contemporaries. The first movement deviates in none of its parts from the sonata-type; in the Scherzo there is nothing novel but the double repeat; the Adagio is a straightforward *Lied* in seven well-defined sections; and the Finale a theme with six variations,* divided into two groups of three by the exposition of the religious chant. But the value, the importance and the proportion of the elements chosen by the singer of the love of mankind, long ago — very long ago — put to rout those who, having ears, hear not.

THE MISSA SOLEMNIS. — We stand in the presence of one of the greatest masterworks in the realm of music. Only works like Bach's Mass in *B* minor, and Wagner's *Parsifal*, can be compared with it. During four consecutive years Beethoven constructed this prodigious monument; "he seems as though transfigured by it," say those who approached him. He dwells above terrestrial contingencies, and he knows that he is writing on a divine text. He has had the sense and the accentuation of the Latin words of the Holy Sacrifice minutely explained to him. He is armed to compose the sublime hymn of prayer, of glory, of love and of peace, to which he adds the epigraph: "Coming from the heart, may it go to the heart."

Should the Missa solemnis be regarded as liturgical music?

---

* There is good reason for surprise that, among the historians of the symphonies, not one has mentioned the mistake left by Beethoven five measures before the fifth variation (*Allegro non tanto*), or, indeed, that which still remains in the Seventh Symphony (first movement, eighth measure of the second exposition). Nevertheless, it would seem that historical comment on such errors is within the province of musicography.

Let us answer boldly, No! This admirable art would surely not be in place in church. Quite out of proportion to the ceremonies of the divine office, the Mass requires the employment of a considerable orchestra, hardly suited for the music appropriate to a place of worship.

Not liturgical music; — but sacred music of the loftiest rank, and, furthermore, essentially Catholic music. We are very far from regarding with suspicion the good faith of those among Beethoven's historiographers who have sought to attach to this unique monument of religious art a purely philosophical significance — to set this Mass down as a work outside of Christian belief, as a manifestation of free thought (they have gone as far as that!); but not to recognize the very spirit of Catholicism in the tenderness wherewith the divine personages are enveloped, in the emotion accompanying the announcement of the mysteries, is in itself proof of blindness — or ignorance.

How can one venture — even had the author not taken pains to tell us clearly — to assert that this entire Mass is not an ardent "act of faith," that this Credo does not proclaim on every page "I believe, not merely in a vague divinity, but in the God of the gospel and in the mysteries of the incarnation, the redemption, and the life eternal"? How gainsay the penetrating emotion — so new in music — which attends these affirmations, and which springs solely from a Catholic comprehension of these dogmas and mysteries? How, finally, can one misconstrue the piously meticulous care with which the sacred words are treated and translated into music, and the marvelous meaning of the expressive accents which unveil their signification to those who can and will understand? For the rest, it suffices to know and to feel, in order to be convinced. We shall endeavor to bring this knowledge home to the reader, hoping to inspire within him that sentiment for beauty and truth to which Beethoven himself laid claim when he wrote to Streicher: "My chief design when writing the Mass was to arouse *religious emotion* in singers and auditors alike, and to render this emotion lasting."

From the beginning of the Kyrie one receives an impression of grandeur which finds an equal only in that given by the similar entry in Bach's great *B*-minor Mass. It is the whole human race that implores divine clemency. The tonality is speedily inflected to the relative minor; a sort of distressful march shows us the Son of God come down to earth; but the word *Christe,* grounded on the same music as *Kyrie,* symbolizes the identity of the two Persons in one God; whereas the third *Kyrie,* representing the Holy Ghost, the third Person participating in the same divinity as the two others, is based upon the third harmonic function, the subdominant, as a bond of union for the three representations of the single God.

The Gloria enters with impressive brilliancy in a trumpet-fanfare confided to the contralti of the chorus. It is important to bring out this typical motive with due effect amid the din of the orchestra; the conductor should see to this. After the shout of glory, all suddenly grows calm on the words *pax hominibus,* etc.; and one can already trace the sketch, in its essential features, of the grand theme of Peace with which the work ends. We cannot dwell on each phrase of the Gloria; but we shall mention, in passing, in the *Gratias agimus tibi,* the emergence of a melodic design later to be cherished by Richard Wagner, principally in the *Meister-*

singer and the *Walküre*. The trumpet-signal which serves
as a pivot for the whole piece, is almost constantly in evidence; every time, at least, that the words imply an appeal
to force or a symbol of power. We may regret that the final
fugue on *in gloria Dei Patris* is not more unlike its congeners,
and develops with no more of interest than the fugues written
by the Kapellmeister of the period on the same words. It is
the weak point of the work.

With the Credo, we reënter the cathedral, not to leave it
again. And what is this Credo, even plastically considered,
but a real cathedral; this sublime monument of Catholic
faith, so strikingly divided into three naves, the central nave
ending with the sacrificial altar "Et homo factus est"? —
The architectural arrangement is a marvel of construction,
a miracle of harmonious, nay, mystical equilibrium. Judge
for yourselves.

The Credo is planned in three grand divisions, following
the *trinitarian* system customary in a great number of liturgical works.

The first division, an exposition of faith in one God, in
itself comprises two affirmations: "I believe in one God,
the Father Almighty," and "in one Lord Jesus Christ."
Both are established in the principal key of $B\flat$ major, with
a transition to the subdominant; after which the two Persons are reunited, on *consubstantialem Patri*, in the tonic.

The second division presents the Evangelical drama of
Jesus descended to earth. It consists of three acts: The
Incarnation, going over to the tonality of *D* major (which
is that of the synthesis of the Mass) on the words *Et homo
factus est;* the scene of the Passion ("Crucifixus"), beginning in *D* major and progressing in depression on the words

of the burial; and the Resurrection, which of a sudden soars upward to the luminous dominant, F major.

The third division is consecrated to the Holy Ghost. Like the first, it contains two subdivisions: The affirmation of belief with regard to the Holy Ghost and the dogmas of the Church; and the celebration of the mystery of eternal life. All this last part does not leave the tonality of the piece.

And there may be found critics so superficial as to assert that the theological sense of the sacred text was a matter of indifference to Beethoven!

We cannot enter into a detailed analysis, for everything would have to be quoted. Let us study only the central portion — the drama. Succeeding the *Incarnatus*, written in the first Gregorian mode, there begins the awful ascent of Calvary. We can follow the Saviour's faltering steps, so rudely underscored by the orchestra. And now there arises, under the bows of the first violins, the moan of the most moving plaint, the sublimest expression of suffering, that ever issued from musician's heart; a plaint yet more intense than the sorrowful melody in Op. 110, in that here it expresses, not human suffering, but the anguish of a God made man. The final fugue is altogether of admirable luminosity. It requires a *very slow* movement; for it should be remembered that when Beethoven writes in $\frac{3}{2}$ time, or even in $\frac{6}{4}$ (as, for instance, in the overture to *Egmont*, the twentieth variation in Op. 120, the religious theme in the Finale of the Ninth Symphony, etc.), he attributes to this notation a signification of majestic slowness; no exception to this rule can be found in his works. This fugue — as regular, with its *stretti*, its *contrary motion* and *diminutions*, as the finest fugues of Bach — is a model of masterful poesy. It might be called a representation of the joys of heaven, as they were imagined by Lippi or Giovanni da Fiesole. It is, in fact, like a fresco from the golden age translated into music; the fancy depicts a mystic dance, a roundel of the blessed pressing with naked feet the flowerets of the celestial meadows. It sounds afar off, this majestic round, scarce to be heard. It approaches, it is close at hand, we are entwined in its hallowed circles — it departs, wellnigh vanishes, but only to return as with an augmented host, yet more enthusiastic, to bear us away in its whirl and to subside, in adoration, before the throne of the Almighty!

Before leaving this Credo it will be interesting to recall a bizarre criticism formulated by certain historiographers with regard to the sentence *Credo in unam sanctam catholicam et apostolicam Ecclesiam.* For the reason that the words of this sentence were entrusted to the tenors only (do not forget that the *tenor* has always been the most important voice in the choir) the inference has been drawn that Beethoven "dodged" this article *because he did not believe in it!* Precisely the opposite seems to us to be the case; for, first of all, each of the preceding articles is treated in the same manner, and one surely can not accuse the spiritually minded Beethoven of wishing to "dodge" the Holy Ghost! So it must be admitted that those critics or *littérateurs* who expressed the above opinion, had read very few Masses; otherwise they might have noticed that both in the liturgical masses of Palestrina and others, and in the most modern masses (we mean those where the text has an influence on the music), this portion of the Credo is always sacrificed, not to say "dodged." Must we suspect Palestrina of unbelief in the dogmas of the Church? The matter is

Cimetière de
Währing
17 Juin 1880.

BEETHOVEN'S FIRST TOMB, AT THE CEMETERY AT WÄHRING

From a sketch made by Vincent d'Indy in 1880

much more simple; one has only to read, with some little attention, the words "Who with the Father and the Son together is worshipped and glorified; Who spake by the Prophets: And I believe one Catholic and Apostolic Church, etc.," to see that *they are not musical.* These words, directed especially against the heresiarchs, do not lend themselves in any way to a lyric or dramatic flight. One believes them, of course, but music is powerless to endow them with expression. Hence, unless one should prefer to set them to an air of conventional type (Bach's way of meeting the difficulty), one must perforce employ psalmody. Such has been the procedure of nearly all composers of masses, and Beethoven makes no exception.

In the Sanctus, Beethoven, respecting the Catholic liturgy and knowing that, during the mystery of the consecration, no voice should make itself heard, Beethoven, by the might of his genius, has raised silence into sublimity. This *praeludium,* which allows the celebrant time to consecrate the elements, is to our mind an inspiration infinitely loftier in conception than the charming concerto for violin and voice which follows. This *praeludium* is admirable in every aspect! What grandeur of *religious* art! — and obtained by means so simple as to be astonishing, did not enthusiasm in this case overwhelm astonishment.

We have now reached the Agnus Dei, that division of the work which we should consider the finest, and the most eloquent of genius, had not the Credo preceded it.

It is here, and in the prelude for the consecration, that Beethoven's religious feeling is most clearly in evidence. The whole long entrance-section, wherein mankind implores the pity of the divine Lamb, is of a beauty still unequalled in musical history. Careful examination will show how greatly this supplication in *Latin*, that is to say, endowed with a peculiarly Catholic expression, differs from the Greek prayer of the Kyrie; — a prayer more carefully ordered, it is true, after the manner of antique art, but less affecting and less urgent. And that the accents of this appeal rise so brokenly toward the throne of the Lamb, the victim of Hate, is because it beseeches Him for peace, "peace *within* and *without*," wrote Beethoven. No more hateful thoughts, no more soul-conflicts or profound dejection; the theme of Peace has emerged, calm and luminous, out of the irresolute key of *B* minor, and has at last given us back the tonality of *D* major, that of Faith and of Love, that wherein the Love of all Mankind is enwreathed in the Ninth Symphony. This theme takes on a pastoral character which gives the impression of a walk in the fields; for Peace is not in the city — it is by the brooks of the valley, among the trees of the forest, that the restless towndweller must seek her; for Peace is not of the world, therefore it is beyond the world that the artist's heart goes forth on her quest: *Sursum corda!*

A simple, quite regular fugue-exposition prepares the blossoming of the peaceful Flower, this affirmative theme which, descending straight from heaven, bears witness that the soul has finally won the enjoyment of that so longed-for peace. This *four*-measure theme appears only four times in the Agnus, but is of such penetrating charm that the spirit of the hearer is left, as it were, impregnated with its perfume, and still feels its spell long after the tones have died away.*

* The penetrative power of this melody is due, technically speaking, to the fact, that, of the nine notes of which it is formed, not one stands on a degree previously heard; thus the melodic design is new in all its elements.

Suddenly — in homage to the traditional *in tempore belli* of Haydn's masses — distant drums and trumpets twice announce the army of Hate. And the soul is anew seized with dread; again it implores; it begs for the promised peace as yet but transiently felt: "We must pray, pray, pray."* But it cannot gain peace without conquering itself. This is the musical apology of Christian renunciation. The theme of peace is transformed; a conflict in the human heart is introduced in the course of the extraordinary orchestral *Presto* in which the peace-motive turns upon itself in a self-annihilating struggle brought to a close by a victorious fanfare. "Above all, the power of the peace within: — Victory!" And here we find the one point whence are derived all the arguments going to show that the Missa solemnis is an exclusively human work, bare of religious spirit; — a *layman's* Mass. "What!" we are told, "a military signal, and twice repeated, at that! It is an opera; it has nothing to do with religion."—And without further ceremony the label *irreligious* is plastered on the Mass! — This reasoning is as just as that which would adduce the bird-songs in the Pastoral Symphony to prove a lack of internal feeling for nature in that symphony — "Empfindung," as Beethoven says — and make it a purely descriptive work. Ancient sophism always consisted in taking *the part for the whole.* And wherein — to speak plainly — does this episode of an appeal to arms, giving way, after a short though bitter struggle, to an ardent prayer, conflict with the religious spirit of the Mass? On the contrary, this fight against the spirit of Hate within us, so destructive of peace, a fight already depicted in the Ninth Symphony in almost the same musical forms, realizes one of the most

* Written, in Beethoven's hand, on his sketches.

[125]

familiar traditional conditions of Christian life. And Beethoven, writing to Count Dietrichstein, the Intendant of the
imperial music, "It is not necessary to follow habitual usage
when the purpose is sincere adoration of God," does he not
himself declare that, if the Mass in D is not liturgical, it was
at least dictated by a religious spirit beyond question? The
episode in whose behalf we have just made this digression is
therefore simply and solely a vital commentary on the words;
the distressful "Have mercy upon us! — upon us, whom the
demons of Hate assail from every side," gives way to the
confident appeal, "Give peace unto our souls!"

And, in truth, it is Peace that anew intervenes. Tender,
radiant Peace waxes like a miraculous plant, and while far-
away drums are beating the retreat of the spirits of Evil,
there spreads for the last time from the height of its upraised
stem the brilliant bloom of the four incomparable measures,
as if to exhale heavenward the perfume of the grateful soul's
act of faith. Is there anything more beautiful in the realm
of music? — And, for the expression of peace won by God's
aid, can one imagine a more sublime offering from a human
being to his divine Creator?

At the present time, when Fashion prescribes to those who
are harnessed to her car a legitimate adulation of the moderns, coupled with an unjust and systematic disparagement
of the old masters, — in this dawn of the century, when some
are seeking to put away Beethoven's art and overcoat in the
glass case for relics, precisely as they have catalogued Haydn's
perruque, and tried to shut up the Wagnerian drama, we
cannot better conclude this essay than by quoting the fine

apostrophe of Suarès on the *Colleone* of Verocchio — a quotation equally applicable to the figure of Beethoven.

"There is nothing in common," writes M. Suarès,* "between this proud, impassioned, believing hero, of a charm rendered poignant through strife, and the mediocre herd that babbles at his feet, or the Barbarians who turn up their pointed noses in his presence. He is unique of his kind. None is his peer, nor does he flatter himself that 'tis so. With falcon-eye he throws a sidelong glance on all around him, a glance that circles over the heads of these petty folk as the hawk poised above his fowls. Let these people crawl about his pedestal, or pass by without seeing him. He has lived — and he lives!"

Ay, of a surety he lives, our grand Beethoven. His masterworks, brought forth in sorrow according to Biblical law, conducted him through sadness and suffering, as he himself sàid, to the possession here below of the joy within the heart, to the peace of those blessed souls who have joined with so great love in the song of his sublime *Credo*.

May his example be of profit to us, and may devotion to his art hasten the reign among us of sweet peace and the bountiful love of all mankind.

March the 21st, 1911.

* Suarès, "Voyage du Condottiére vers Venise."

A METHODICAL AND CHRONOLOGICAL LIST OF BEETHOVEN'S WORKS

I. YOUTHFUL COMPOSITIONS (1782–1793)

Year	For Orchestra	Op.	Chamber Music	Op.	Piano (Organ, Harp)	Op.	Lieder	Op.
1782					9 Variations on a march by Dressler (C minor). Fugue for Org., with 2 themes. 7 Bagatelles, 1st version of op. 33 (see 1802).		Schilderung eines Mädchens.	
1783					Minuet (E♭). Rondo (C). 3 Sonatas (E♭, F min., D).			
1784	Concerto for Pf. (E♭) (unfinished).				2 Sonatinas (G, F) (?). Rondo (A) (?).		An einen Säugling.	
1785			3 Quartets for Pf. Vn. Va. Vo. (E♭, D, C) (sketches).					
1786			Trio for Pf., Flute and Bassoon.		Prelude (F minor).			

	Count v. Waldstein. Cantata for the accession of Emperor Leopold II.	Rondino for 2 Oboes, 2 Clarinets, 2 Horns, 2 Bassoons.		*Der freie Mann*, 1st version (see 1797). 2 Airs to Umlauf's operetta *Die schöne Schusterin*. 2 Airs: *Prüfung des Kusses* and *Mit Mädeln sich vertragen*.
1791				
1792	2 Trios for Pf. Vn. Vo. (B♭, E♭). Trio for Vn. Va. Vo., 1st version of op. 3 (see 1796) (E♭).			
	Allegro and Minuet for 2 Flutes (?). March for 2 Clars, 2 Horns, 2 Bassoons. Sonata for Pf. and Flute. Rondo for Pf. and Vn. (G). Octet for 2 Oboes, 2 Clarinets, 2 Horns, 2 Bassoons, 1st version of the Quintet, op. 4 (see 1797). Variations for Pf. and Vn. on "Se vuol ballare," from Mozart's *Le Nozze di Figaro*. Variations for Pf. Vn. Vo. on an original theme (E♭). 103	13 Variations on Dittersdorf's "Es war einmal ein alter Mann" (A). Variations for 4 hands on a theme by Count v. Waldstein.		*Elegie auf den Tod eines Pudels. Ich, der bisher ein Feind der Liebe war.* .... 50 *Feuerfarbe. Urian's Reise.*

NOTE. — Works marked (?) are those whose authorship is uncertain. The works are arranged chronologically according to the dates on which they were finished, and not according to the years of publication.

II. FIRST PERIOD (1792–1801)

Year	For Orchestra	Op.	Chamber Music	Op.	Piano	Op.	Lieder	Op.
1793			3 Trios for Pf. Vn. Vo., to Prince Lichnowsky (E♭, G, C)	1				
1794	Concerto for Pf. (B♭), 1st version of op. 19 (see 1800). Rondo for Pf. (B♭) (unfinished).				Minuet (A♭). Variations on the quintet in Paisiello's *Molinara*.		*Opferlied* (Matthison), 1st version.	
1795	12 Minuets. 12 Allemandes. 6 Minuets. Concerto for Pf. (D), 1st movement.				Variations on the duet in Paisiello's *Molinara*; "Nel corpù non mi sento." Variations on a minuet in Haibl's *Le Nozze disturbate*. 3 Sonatas (F minor, A, C), to Haydn. Sonatina (C), to Eleonore von Breuning (unfinished).	**2**		
1796			Trio for Vn. Va. Vo., 2d version (see 1791). 2 Sonatas for Pf. and Vo. (F, G minor). Serenade for Vn. Va. Vo. 12 Variations (G) for Pf. and Vo. on the march from Händel's *Judas Maccabæus*. Sextet for 2 Horns, 2 Vn. Va. Vo., 1st version of op.	3 5 8	Variations on a Russian dance in Branitzky's *Waldmädchen*. 7 Ländler (slow waltzes). Sonata for 4 hands (D). Sonata (E♭) to Babette v. Keglevich. Sonata (G). Rondo (C).	6 7 49² 51¹	*Adelaide* (Matthison). *Seufzer eines Ungeliebten*, and *Gegenliebe* (Bürger). *Abschiedsgesang an Wien's Bürger*, terzetto. *Ah! perfido!* scene and aria.	46 65

Year	No.	Work	No.	Work	No.	Work	Notes
			16	Quintet for Pf., Oboe, Clarinet, Bassoon and Horn (E♭). (Orig. transcription for Pf. Vn. Va. Vo.).		8 Variations on Grétry's "Une fièvre brûlante" (C).	solo and chorus.
			9	3 Trios for Vn. Va. Vo. (G, D, C).		7 Variations on Winter's "Kind, willst du ruhig schlafen," (F).	Gretels Warnung (Goethe), 1st version of op. 75 (see 1809).
			66	Variations for Pf. and Vo. on "Ein Mädchen oder Weibchen," from Mozart's Magic Flute.		10 Variations on "La stessa, la stessissima," from Salieri's Falstaff (B♭).	Der freie Mann, 2d version (see 1790).
			71	Sextet for 2 Clarinets, 2 Horns, 2 Bassoons (E♭).			La Partenza (Metastasio).
			87	Trio for 2 Oboes and Cor anglais (C).			
1798			11	Trio for Pf., Clarinet and Vo. (B♭).		8 Variations on a trio by Süssmayer, "Tändeln und scherzen," (F).	Ich denke Dein (Andenken).
			12	3 Sonatas for Pf. and Vn. (D, A minor, E♭) to Salieri.	10	3 Sonatas (C min., F, D).	Ich liebe Dich (?).
						Sonata (C) pathétique.	
					13 14	2 Sonatas (D, G).	
1799	21	First Symphony (C), to Baron van Swieten.	18	6 Quartets for Vn. Vn. Va. Vo., to Prince Lobkowitz.	49¹	Sonata (G).	
			20	Grand Septet for Clarinet, Horn, Bassoon, Vn. Va. Vo. and Bass.			
1800	19 37	(2d) Concerto for Pf. (B♭), 2d version (see 1794). 3d Concerto for Pf. (C).	17	Sonata for Pf. and Horn (F).	22	Sonata (B♭).	
	43	Die Geschöpfe des Prometheus, Ballet-music.			51²	6 Variations for 4 hands on theme of Lied Andenken. Rondo (G).	

III. SECOND PERIOD (1801–1815)

Year	For Orchestra	Op.	Chamber Music	Op.	Piano	Op.	Lieder	Op.
1801			Sonata for Pf. and Vn. (A minor).	23	Sonata (D), *pastorale*.	28	Canon, *Lob auf den Dicken*, to Schuppanzigh.	
			Sonata for Pf. and Vn. (F).	24	Sonata (Ab).	28	*Der Wachtelschlag* (The Skylark).	
			Serenade for Flute, Vn. Va.	25	*Sonata quasi fantasia* (E).	27		
			(2d) Quintet for Vn. Vn. Va. Va. Vo.	29	*Sonata quasi fantasia* (C# minor) to Giulietta Guicciardi.	27		
1802	Second Symphony (D), to Prince Lichnowsky.	36	3 Sonatas for Pf. and Vn., to Emperor Alexander (A, C minor, G).	30	Sonata (G).	31	*An die Hoffnung* (Tiedge).	32
	Christ on the Mount of Olives, Oratorio.	85	6 Ländler (slow waltzes) for 2 Vns. and Vo.		Sonata (D).	31	6 Songs (Gellert) for Soprano.	48
			12 Contredanses for 2 Vns. and Vo.		7 Bagatelles, 2d version (see 1782).	33	*Das Glück der Freundschaft*.	88
			Sonata (D) for Pf. and Flute, after the Serenade op. 25.	41	6 Variations (F) on an original theme.	34	Terzetto, *Tremate, empj*.	116
					Variations and Fugue on a theme from the ballet *Prometheus*, op. 43.	35		
1803	Romance for Violin (G).	40	Sonata for Pf. and Vn., to Kreutzer (A).	47	Sonata (Eb).	31		
	Romance for Violin (F).	50	Noturno for Pf. and Va. (D) arrd. from the Serenade op. 8.	42	March of the Emperor Alexander (?).			
			Variations for Pf. Vn. Vo. (Eb?).	44	3 Marches for 4 hands.			
					7 Variations on "God save the King" (C).			
					5 Variations on "Rule Britannia" (D).			
1804	Third Symphony (Eb), *Eroica*.	55			Sonata (F), *appassionata*.	57		
					Sonata (D), *Waldstein*.	53		
					Andante (F) from op. 53.			
					Sonata (F).	54		
1805	*Fidelio* (*Leonore*), Opera in 3 acts, 1st version.	72						
	Overture to *Leonore* No. 1 (C).	138						
	Triple Concerto for Pf. Vn. Vo.	56						
	4th Concerto for Pf. (G).	58						
1806	Overture to *Leonore* No. 2 (C).	72	3 Quartets for Vn. Vn. Va. Vo. (F, E minor, C), to Count Rasoumowsky.	59	32 Variations (C) on an original theme.		*Als die Geliebte* (Lydien's Untreue).	
	Fourth Symphony (Bb) to Count Oppersdorf.	60						
	Concerto for Violin (D).	61						
1807	Concerto for Pf. (D), original		Transcription for trio of the quintet	63			*Sehnsucht* (Goethe and Reissiger, 4 settings of the same	

Year	No.		No.		No.		No.	
(cont.)	68 80	…ride, to Prince Lobkowitz and Count Rasoumowsky. Fantasia for Pf., orchestra and chorus.						
1809	73	Fifth Concerto for Pf. (E♭).	74 81	10th Quartet for Vn. Vn. Va. Vo. (E♭), to Prince Lobkowitz. Sextet for 2 Horns, Vn. Vn. Va. Vo., 2d version (see 1796).	76 77 79 78 81	6 Variations (D) (1st sketch of the "Ruins of Athens" march). Fantaisie (G minor). Sonata (G). Sonata (F♯), to the Countess of Brunswick. Sonata (E♭), l'adieu, l'absence, le retour, to Archduke Rudolph.	75 82 83 122	6 Lieder (Goethe and Reissiger). 4 Ariettas and 1 Duet. 3 Lieder (Goethe). Lied aus der Ferne. Der Laute Klage. Der Liebende. Gedenke mein. Der Jüngling in der Fremde.
1810	84	Overture to *Egmont*, and the incidental music to Goethe's tragedy. 2 Marches for military band, (F), to Archduke Anton. Polonaise for military band.	95	11th Quartet for Vn. Vn. Va. Vo. (F minor), to Zmeskall von Domanowecz.				Irish Songs, with Pf. Vn. and Vo.
1811	113 114 117	Overture to *The Ruins of Athens*. *The Ruins of Athens*: incidental music to Kotzebue's drama. *King Stephen*, overture and incidental music to Kotzebue's drama.	97	Trio for Pf. Vn. Vo. (B♭), to Archduke Rudolph.				*An die Geliebte*: 2 settings.
1812	92 93	Seventh Symphony (A), to Count Fries. Eighth Symphony (F).	96	Trio (in one movement), to Maximilienne Brentano. Sonata for Pf. and Vn. (G). 3 Equali for 4 Trombones, written for All Saints' Day.				
1813	91	Triumphal March for Kuffner's *Tarpeja* (C). *Wellington's Victory*, or *The Battle of Vittoria*.		6 Allemandes for Pf. and Vn. (F, D, F, A, D, G).				Canon. *Kurz ist der Schmerz*, 1st version. *Der Bardengeist.*
1814	72 72 115 136 118	*Fidelio*, opera in 2 acts (2d revised version). Overture to *Fidelio* (E). Overture in C ("*Namensfeier*") for the Emperor's name-day. Melodramatic music for Duncker's drama *Prohaska*. Cantata *Germania* (4 parts). Cantata *Der glorreiche Augenblick*, for the Vienna Congress. (Elegiac Song) for 4 parts and strings, in memory of Baroness Pasqualati.		3 Duos for Clarinet and Bassoon (C, F, B♭).	89 90	Polonaise in C. Sonata in E, to Count Lichnowsky.	100	Chorus, *Ihr, weise Gründer.* *Gute Nachricht.* *Kriegers Abschied.* *Abschiedsgesang*, to Tucher. *Merkenstein*, Duet. *Cantata campestre.* *Un lieto brindisi*, a 4, to Mal-latti. Canon *Kurz ist der Schmerz*, 2d version.

IV. THIRD PERIOD (1815-1827)

Year	For Orchestra	Op.	Chamber Music	Op.	Piano	Op.	Lieder	Op.
1815	Cantata *Meeresstille u. glück-liche Fahrt.* *Es ist vollbracht,* chorus for Treitschke's poem.	112	2 Sonatas for Pf. and Vn., to Countess v. Erdödy (C, D). Original transcription for string-quintet of the trio op. 1, No. 3	102, 104			*An die Hoffnung.* 25 Scotch Songs with Pf. Vn. and Vo. Song to Reissig's "Sehnsucht," *Die stille Nacht.* *Das Geheimniss.* 2 Canons: *Das Reden, Das Schweigen.*	94, 108
1816	Cantata for Prince Lobkowitz. 2 Marches for military band (D).				Sonata in A, to Baroness Ertmann.	101	*Ruf vom Berge.* 6 Songs (Liederkreis) *An die ferne Geliebte.* *Der Mann von Wort.*	98, 99
1817			Fugue for string-quintet (Vn. Vn. Va. Va. Vo.) (D).	137			*So oder so, Nord oder Süd.* Monks' Song from Schiller's *Wilhelm Tell,* to the memory of Krumpholz. *Resignation.* Canon, *Ta, ta, ta,* to Maelzel (see 8th symphony).	
1818					Andante maestoso (C), called "Beethoven's Last Thought." Sonata in Bb, to Archduke Rudolph.	106	*O Hoffnung* (chorus). 12 Folksongs (for 3 parts). Canon, *Ich bin bereit.*	
1819					6 themes, varied with Flute or Vn. *ad lib.* 10 Folk-songs, varied, Russian, Scotch, Tyrolese, w. Flute *ad lib.*	105, 107	Cantata, *Glaube und hoffe,* to Schlesinger. Wedding-song, *Auf! Freunde,* to Gian. del Rio. Canon, *Glück zum neuen Jahr,* to Mme. von Erdödy.	
1820					12 easy Bagatelles, for Starke. Sonata in E minor, to Maximilienne Brentano	119, 109	*Abendlied.* Canon, *Alles Gute,* to Archduke Rudolph.	

1822	Missa solemnis (D), to Archduke Rudolph. 123 Overture Zur Weihe des Hauses 124 Gratulations-Menuett			Sonata in C minor, to Archduke Rudolph. 111 6 Bagatelles. 126 Rondo (G), "The Lost Groschen". 129	Der Kuss (Weisse). 128
1823	Ninth Symphony (D), to Frederick Wm. II, king of Prussia. 125		Adagio and 10 Variations (G) for Pf. Vn. Vo., on Müller's "Ich bin der Schneider Kakadu". 121	33 Variations (C) on a waltz by Diabelli. 120	Opferlied (Matthison); 3d version (see 1794 and 1797), for Soprano, chorus and wind-instruments. 121 Canon, a 6, Edel sei der Mensch (Goethe). Canon, a 5, Falstafferel, to Schuppanzigh. Canon, Ich bitte dich, dedicated to Hauschka. Canon, Bester Graf, Sie sind ein Schaf, to Count Lichnowsky. Canon, Te solo adoro. 122 Bundeslied a 2
1824		12th Quartet (Eb), for Vn. Vn. Va. Vo., to Prince Galitzin. 127			
1825		15th Quartet (A minor), for Vn. Vn. Va. Vo., to Prince Galitzin. 132 13th Quartet (Bb), for Vn. Vn. Va. Vo., to Prince Galitzin. 130 Grand Fugue, for Vn. Vn. Va. Vo., to Archduke Rudolph. 133 Original transcription of the Grand Fugue op. 133 for Pf. 4 hands. 134			Canon: Schwenke. " Bogen. " Signor abbate. " Ewig Dein. " Freue Dich des Lebens. " Doctor, sperrt das Thor dem Tod. " Kühl, nicht lau. " Si non per portas. " Ars longa. " Wir irren alle.
1826		14th Quartet (C# minor), for Vn. Vn. Va. Vo., to Baron von Stutterheim. 131 16th Quartet (F), for Vn. Vn. Va. Vo., to Johann Wolfmeier. 135 Andante in G, from sketches for a quintet.			